EMILY IN PARIS

VORACIOUS

LITTLE, BROWN AND COMPANY
New York Boston London

Contents

Bonjour!

I have *always* been in love with glamour. My hometown was pretty ordinary so I got my shot of luxury, glamour and chic from the movies I watched, the gorgeous stars from Hollywood's golden age (hello, Audrey Hepburn) and the amazing lifestyles I saw on TV shows like *Gossip Girl*. I couldn't get enough of it. I bet most of you can relate. I just adored the poetry of what we can do with words, pictures and stories, and how we can spin them into dreams. As soon as I could, I headed for the big city – Chicago – to get a job in marketing that would give me a chance to use those tools to reach people – and the best way, my way, was social media. I love conversation! I love friends. I love to talk and I love to share. What better way to do that than via Instagram, Twitter and Facebook, where one post can reach millions of people?

So when I got my marketing job with the Gilbert Group, where I could do what I enjoyed all day long, I thought I had it made. I was doing pretty well in Chicago. I had my job and I loved my boss, Madeline, who also loved me. I had a great boyfriend and we were engaged to be engaged. My life was going to be happy and down-the-line ordinary, with ball games, beers, backyards and then motherhood – cheering on my kids from the sidelines, making lunches and cooking up dinners. It was going to be wholesome and it was going to be great.

Until Paris.

My life began in Paris. My real life, I mean.

#EmilyinParis

In Paris I learned about a million different ways to live, most of them completely baffling. I mean, come on – I will never understand why the first floor is the ground floor and the second floor is the first floor – that is just weird. I'm sorry, it is. But I suppose if I hadn't kept on getting it wrong, then I wouldn't have met Gabriel, who was probably my first friend in Paris. I don't know how I managed to end up with a studio apartment right above the hottest chef in town, but I did.

Speaking of where I live, maybe you'd like to know a little bit about it. My area is the Panthéon, named after the famous mausoleum where France's most celebrated citizens are buried. It's a huge honor to be interred there and it holds the remains of great men like Voltaire and Victor Hugo (who wrote *Les Misérables*) and a ton of famous politicians. More than seventy men are represented, but only six women, so come on, French ladies! You need to get on with being buried in the Panthéon and even things up a bit. The last woman to join the club was Josephine Baker, who was black and a famous dancer and singer, so that is amazingly cool. Some real glamour in there, at last.

The Panthéon is in the 5th arrondissement. The arrondissements are like the zones of the town, or the boroughs, but to be properly French, they have to be completely out of order. Don't expect to find the fourth next to the fifth, that would be waaay too easy. The French want to baffle you, it's part of their mission. That's why I felt like *Alice Through the Looking Glass* for weeks when I first arrived here.

The 5th arrondissement is not as chic as some but I soon grew to love it. My square, the Place de l'Estrapade, has a beautiful fountain in the middle of it, cobbled streets and ancient lampposts. It looks like something out of the *Madeline* books. Quintessentially Parisian apartment buildings border the square, with their tall windows, little balconies and, hidden behind the front gates, private courtyard gardens. Each one has a twisting staircase up to the many floors (there is rarely an elevator but that is so good for the calf muscles that I don't mind) and is ruled over by a *concièrge*, which is the French word for janitor. French *concièrges* are even more grumpy and impossible than American janitors, who can at least tell you to get lost in English, and they make it a point of honor to speak French loudly and very fast, especially if they know you can't understand.

Right at the top is my tiny apartment, known as a *chambre de bonne*, a maid's room, from where I can look out over the rooftops like Nicole Kidman in *Moulin Rouge*.

Anyway, the Panthéon is a beautiful area and if you visit it, you must go to my favorite bakery, La Boulangerie Moderne, and get a *pain au chocolat* and eat it as you walk along the cobbled streets, and let the butter and chocolate melt on your tongue. OMG. I realized on the spot that butter + chocolate = bliss. You must try. I insist. Take a picture and Instagram it, and please, please hashtag me so I see it.

Everything is taken seriously in Paris. Food, *bien sûr* (of course), and wine. Fashion – well, Paris is where fashion began so … *bien sûr* as well. It's the home of Chanel, Givenchy, Dior, and of course the great Pierre Cadault, and it is where haute couture was created. No one thinks that fashion is frivolous or silly or a waste of time, and anyone who does might be a snob, so watch out for that. I have lots of tips for my favorite styles and fashion finds in here, and my top places to shop too.

Then there's ART. Parisians love art like a religion, and that includes literature, ballet, opera, theater, architecture and all the rest, and they don't consider you even vaguely worth noticing unless you know something about these things. It's not all highbrow, though. Parisians also take fun seriously, because they believe that life is to be lived, and work and fun must balance almost evenly. There is a lot of fun to be had in Paris, and I'll tell you some of my favorite places to go for a riotous night out, particularly if you are in the company of a famous and drunk movie star.

We ought to mention sex. People are unashamedly obsessed with sex in Paris, and they celebrate it too. Everyone should be having it, it's almost a rule. They think it's as natural as eating dinner, and just as necessary. I kind of love that. Parisians are buttoned-up in some ways, and completely unbuttoned in others.

Beauty is worshiped in Paris. Style in all its forms. But most of all – they love LOVE. Paris is a city for lovers, the most romantic place in the world. Around every corner is somewhere gorgeous and Instagrammable. If you want a romantic kiss, you are spoiled for choice (but I have some ideas inside). It can never, never grow old and there is nothing like the magical light of Paris, by day or by night. *#cityoflight*

And that's why, in Paris, I began to live. Really live. Now I'm going to tell you some of what I learned about all these things the French take seriously and how they changed me … so read on …

Emily

xoxo

Emily's World

Just in case it's useful, I thought I'd give you some thumbnail sketches of my friends and colleagues here in Paris. These people have completely shaped my experience and I could not have asked for a more wonderful group to be my support system.

GABRIEL

Gabriel was the first person I met in Paris. He's a chef from Normandy, and lives in the apartment below me, which meant I ended up more than once trying to get into his apartment instead of mine because of me just not getting the floor numbering thing. He was kind and welcoming from the first, acting as a translator and happily lending his shower when I needed it. Ambitious, talented and exceptionally hardworking, he was a chef at Les Deux Compères just near the apartment building, but accepted Antoine Lambert's investment and opened his own restaurant, Chez Lavaux, on the same site. Gabriel is ridiculously hot but when I found out he was also the boyfriend of my new friend Camille, I was horrified. I'd just kissed him. I've done my best but sometimes it's impossible to resist him, and we've had two amazing nights of passion which I think means more than it should to both of us. But now he and Camille are reconciled, and I don't know what to do next.

MINDY CHEN

Where would I be without Mindy? My first friend in Paris. I was captivated by her approachability, humor and beauty – along with her cool style – and we were friends at once. My guide to all things French, she's helped me negotiate parties, waiters and life in this confusing city. Mindy arrived in Paris after choking on TV in front of billions of people during an audition for *Chinese Popstar*. When she gave up on business school, Mindy's super-rich father, the zipper king of China, cut her off without a cent. Mindy became a nanny and then, despite an expired visa, let her friend Li talk her into restarting her singing career, first at a drag club and now with a two-piece support band consisting of Étienne and Benoît. Theatrical and exuberant, Mindy has an amazing singing voice and she and Benoît make wonderful music together – in every way. 😛

CAMILLE

Camille is utterly gorgeous, kind and charming. I love her style, classic with a twist, and her sweet friendliness won my heart at once. We would have a perfect friendship if it weren't for the fact she is in love with Gabriel, who has been her boyfriend for the last five years. Camille is the middle of three children: her older brother is Théo and her younger brother is Timothée (who looks older than he is – more about that later). Her parents, Louise and Gérard, produce their own label champagne from their home, Château de Lalisse in Épernay, Champagne. Camille works in an art gallery and also helps run the family business.

SYLVIE GRATEAU

My boss and the managing director of Savoir, Sylvie is incredibly chic, glamorous and impressive. Oh, did I say terrifying? She's also terrifying. Until you get to know her better, when she becomes a tiny bit less terrifying. Sylvie used to be a photographer but now heads up the marketing company left in her care by its owner Paul Brossard. To my amazement, I discovered she is married to Laurent G and was co-owner of his Saint-Tropez restaurant until she sold her share to start her own business. She and

Laurent obviously have an understanding, as Sylvie has been romantically involved with Antoine Lambert, head of Maison Lavaux, and with Erik, a photographer. Smart and successful, Sylvie is fearless, demanding and an inspiration.

LUC

One of the account managers at Savoir, Luc has many passions in his life, but the top ones seem to be sex, chess, and avoiding women called Marianne. Luc has strong ideas about what it means to be French and is keen to protect French ideas, culture and its enthusiasm for a naked actress. Luc has a philosophical streak and is very talented at his job. He was too nice to take part in calling me *La Plouc* – the hick – and has turned out to be one of my best friends and supporters. He enjoys riding his bike, watching French films and picnicking in cemeteries.

JULIEN

Julien was the first person I ever met at Savoir and I soon got used to his expression of puzzled scorn. He is an account director at Savoir and has a passion for brightly colored two-piece suits which he wears with a gold watch chain in the pocket. Super stylish and somewhat temperamental, Julien has a heart of gold and has proved a good friend, often giving me a heads-up about what's going in the office and, most importantly, with Sylvie. We've had our clashes, mostly over managing our accounts, but a lot of laughs too. Now I just want him to find the perfect guy, after my faux pas with regards to him and Benoît...

ALFIE

Alfie is a Brit who was born in Hampshire. He has three brothers and a dog called Clover (I can also say this in French, by the way). He works in financial services connected with overseeing the Brexit transition (OMG, don't ask) and has come to Paris temporarily from his home and job in London. He lives in the business district of La Défense and prefers American food to French food, which I hear isn't usual at all. He doesn't speak French, adores football, and it takes a little while to crack that cynical shell and find the sweet guy inside. Wears good jackets.

GÉRARD, LOUISE, THÉO AND TIMOTHÉE

Camille's family. Like I said, Gérard and Louise run the château and vineyard. Louise does the business work and is very protective of her children, particularly of Camille and her relationship with Gabriel. Gérard is the flamboyant figurehead (the Champère) who likes to cut the top off a champagne bottle with a sword when he's not sunbathing in the nude. Her brothers are very cool (and Timothée is sooo sweet) and they hope to run the business in due course.

ANTOINE LAMBERT

A composer of perfume, Antoine is one of the most highly respected noses in France. He is owner of Maison Lavaux, the perfume house, and is an investor in Chez Lavaux, Gabriel's new restaurant venture. He is married to Catherine but had an affair with Sylvie for some years. Charming and old-fashioned, Antoine has some interesting ideas about what makes a woman powerful – dressing in lacy black underwear, if she gets dressed at all, is one – but I think I've helped him see that the modern woman has got some very different boundaries.

CATHERINE LAMBERT
Antoine's glamorous wife, who knows about his relationship with Sylvie, also made me understand that if I wanted an affair with Antoine, she was cool with that. I will never understand the French!

PIERRE CADAULT
The legendary French fashion designer who had an affair with Elton John and feuded with Valentino and Grégory Duprée. Pierre is notoriously 'creative' and branded me a *ringarde* – basic bitch – when he saw my Eiffel Tower bag charm. It took all my efforts and a shared love of *Gossip Girl* to win him back. After his brand was targeted by Grey Space, a pair of fashion terrorists, and his beautiful dress sprayed with gray paint, I helped him to reinvent himself as a fresh, modern voice, but he is still somewhat temperamental, to say the least. He has a pet iguana called Evangelista (who has now been replaced five times and counting).

MATHIEU CADAULT

Pierre's nephew and business manager Mathieu is a handsome playboy with a string of famous girlfriends and a gorgeous flat overlooking the Seine. He was interested in me for a while but after he heard me on the phone to Gabriel and got the wrong… right… wrong idea, he dropped me at once – but was generous enough to let me take on my own the vacation in Saint-Tropez we were going to have together. We still work together, and are just good friends.

LAURENT G

Laurent is very cool, and is the owner of a beachside bar and restaurant near Saint-Tropez, named after himself. He's also Sylvie's husband, but they have lived separately for years. He has just bought out her share of his business, which will allow Sylvie to set up on her own now that she's left Savoir.

MADELINE WHEELER

My boss from Chicago, language major Madeline unexpectedly got pregnant and so missed out on going to Paris, which was lucky for me. She kept tabs on us all from afar but now she has arrived, she's been determined to impose her American sensibilities on the French company. That has gone down badly. I mean, VERY badly. Like, everyone has walked out. That badly. The great thing is that Madeline doesn't seem to have noticed what a disaster that is.

PAUL BROSSARD

Owner of Savoir who sold the firm to the Gilbert Group, Paul is charming but smokes in the office and thinks Americans are a waste of time, unless they are paying him a fortune for his business!

RANDY ZIMMER

I was pretty excited to meet Randy at Camille's gallery showing. Everyone knows he's a star entrepreneur from Chicago who has founded a chain of luxury hotels across the world, most recently in Paris. Maison Lavaux provides its signature scent. And I managed to impress him with an amazing dinner at Gabriel's restaurant.

THOMAS

A semiotics professor, Thomas was my first French boyfriend. We met at the Café de Flore and he was exactly the kind of Frenchman I expected to meet drinking wine at a bistro table: smart, cultured and sexy. But unfortunately, he was an intellectual snob who looked down on everyone. Gabriel couldn't stand him. It was a sign. I dumped him on the steps of the Palais Garnier in one my finest moments.

BROOKLYN CLARK

Brooklyn is one of my favorite movie stars, but she was not exactly the archetypal American sweetheart when she arrived in Paris to be the face of the Fourtier watch launch. She was sort of rude and entitled, but later warmed up and became pretty

sweet, before disappearing into the night with a 2-million-euro watch and nearly giving me a heart attack. Loves to get high, party and hook up with handsome strangers.

OLIVIA THOMPSON

The icy, impressive and chic British founder and head of cosmetics company Durée. She loves social media and dislikes Sylvie Grateau. She believes that influencers are more important than professional marketers. I guess we'll have to disagree on that one. She was keen to recruit me as a brand ambassador, but I was more interested in persuading her to come back to Savoir as a client … It didn't work out.

GRÉGORY DUPRÉE

A flamboyant fashion designer who adores handsome young men and muscled body builders, Grégory worked with Pierre in the early days but a later feud meant they fell out. He managed to fool me into driving Pierre into a frenzy of Grateau, posing on the suitcase with Pierre's face on it. Thanks, Grégory. I got my own back by inviting myself on his yacht, and a lot of hard work resulted in a crazy fashion show at Versailles, with the two old enemies reconciled. Phew!

GREY SPACE
A pair of fashion terrorists who hijack labels and spaces to make their own anarchic statements, often using gray paint. They bought Pierre's dress at auction, as modeled by me, and then sprayed me with thick gray gloop. But it made me see there are new ways to get attention and we managed to beat them at their own game by Pierre Cadault hijacking their Paris fashion week venue with an amazing stunt.

DOUG
My Chicago boyfriend who couldn't handle a long-distance relationship or the time difference. He seemed to prefer phone sex to the real thing. His decision not to visit Paris showed me that we had no future together and although I was miserable, I knew breaking up was the right thing to do.

BENOÎT
Talented guitarist, singer and composer who fell for Mindy's voice and wrote beautiful songs for her. She thought he was gay and, following my advice, tried to set him up with Julien, so she was astonished when he turned out to be straight. But she liked it. He was prepared to forgive her secret life as a rich girl because he loves her for herself.

ÉTIENNE
A keyboard player from Shanghai, Étienne managed to discover Mindy's secret and outed her as a billionaire's daughter and poor little rich girl. Personally, I think this was mean. But he thought he was doing the right thing, and maybe it was best in the end, even if it was an extreme way to do it.

ERIK
Photographer and lover of Sylvie Grateau, Erik is so sweet-natured and lovely. I think we might be seeing more of him …

EMILY'S FASHION PARIS

Chapter 1

You will not be surprised to learn that I've always loved fashion. I love to express myself through clothes, and I adore color, texture, prints, shape and style.

But most of all I love FUN!

Sometimes I felt I was just a little too quirky for my conservative hometown. Even in cosmopolitan Chicago, they don't always agree that you need to wear a sweet little pink Kenzo dress to promote pharmaceutical and geriatric-care products. But that's exactly the time when you need a lift from amazing clothes the most, right? *#fashionliftsthespirits*

Paris is a city that loves color, style and statements, and of course it's the home of haute couture. As soon as I arrived, I felt liberated to embrace fashion as fully as I could, and although I've always stayed true to myself and my personal style, I couldn't help absorbing a little Parisian flair.

When I started at the marketing company Savoir, my French boss Sylvie didn't seem to appreciate some of my more colorful moments at first. I do love black, but in the daytime I pair it with something strong and contrasting, like neon pink, purple or red. Sassy chic, if you will. I like the unexpected: a flash of plaid or lace or a metallic or camouflage. Clashing patterns. Checks and stripes. Statements.

#fashionliftsthespirits

BOOTS, BELTS, 'BAGAGES', BERETS & BUCKET HATS

Here is my go-to guide to recreating my favorite looks. To add my signature style to your outfits, just remember your four Bs: boots, belts, *bagages* (purses), berets and bucket hats. Is that five Bs? I think berets and bucket hats are both worn on the head, so they are standing in for all hats. I love a hat. Hats add interest and a fresh fashion element. Put a straw coolie hat with jeans and you have a totally different feel.

OK, let's start at the bottom.

BOOTS

Or as the French say, *bottines*.

OMG, I could not live without boots. I love high-heeled ankle boots. My favorites are a pair of plaid Louboutins with glitter highlights that are just as fabulous as they sound. I also have white patent ones with zips and kitten heels, quirky purple patent-leather scalloped-edge ones with square toes that end mid-calf, and shoe-boots with killer stiletto heels. As I got braver in Paris, I tried a pair of boots with even more flair: pink, plastic and transparent.

My best friend Mindy (you'll hear a lot of her in this book) is like me and loves an open-toed shoe-boot with zips up the back. My other close friend Camille doesn't often go for high heels; she loves a flat: chunky loafers, Derbys and lace-up Oxfords. But she brings out the big guns for a crazy night out.

High, barely-there sandals look amazing with a long floaty dress, but you can put your boots with anything. (Boots also protect your feet better from the *merde* on Parisian sidewalks.)

I love my quirky purple patent-leather scalloped-edge ones with square toes that end mid-calf.

OMG, I could not live without my boots!

BELTS

A belt can make an outfit, I'm not exaggerating. And you can get so much use from them, so I definitely advise that you invest in a few good ones. Make sure you have at least one wide black belt that cinches in the waist. A black belt adds interest to a dress and gives it an edge that stops you from looking too cute and girly. I like a belt with studs or texture that contrasts with a feminine, puffy dress.

Sylvie wears big black belts too, which show off her tiny waist. Of course, she doesn't believe in food – more often than not, her lunch is a cigarette (smoked, not eaten, *bien sûr #indulgeme*).

A narrow white belt is a good contrast, but don't be afraid to go for something really powerful: bright red or a purple snakeskin. When in doubt, clash, don't match!

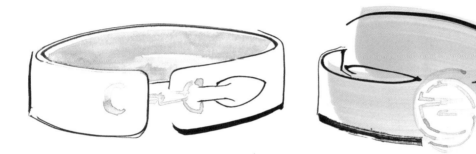

BAGAGES – PURSES

Okay, I'm cheating. *Bagages* actually means luggage. The French word for purse is *sac* but that doesn't sound good at all. Sack? No way does that convey the fun and playfulness of a purse!

You can really enjoy yourself with your purses. If you only need enough room for a phone and a lipstick, then you can have great fun with what you carry. I have an adorable Chanel purse in the shape of an orb, which I love. I mean, you can't put much inside it, but it's so fun and it makes me happy, so who cares? My evening purse, which is a face wearing a pair of sunglasses, cheers me up so much, I can't say.

If you need to carry more, like a laptop or tablet and a charger, you can jazz up a plain bowling bag with a silky ribbon tied around the handles. If you have to carry a big tote, try to color-coordinate with your clothes so that it doesn't look too big. The bulk can disappear against the color of your dress or jacket.

I collect purses in all textures and colors but my absolute favorite is the vintage Chanel purse. Everyone knows they are the last word in chic. The famous classic is the 2.55, so called because it was designed in February 1955, in quilted calfskin leather, with brass hardware: the leather-threaded chain and the iconic, intertwined-C clasp. But you can find the most adorable versions of a Chanel bag in suede, velvet and leather, and in vibrant colors. One of my favorites is a great tan saddlebag with a round coin purse dangling from it. It's so different and I love it.

I can't pretend Chanel bags are cheap, even when they're pre-loved. But they are an investment! I guarantee it. You will find that very often you can sell a genuine designer piece for at least what you paid for it, through a specialist vintage shop or a website dedicated to well-cared-for designer labels.

I can't pretend Chanel bags are cheap, even when they're pre-loved. But they are an investment!

Emily's Tip

Always keep the packages, bags and boxes. Stuff purses with acid-free tissue paper to keep their shape. Keep them clean. Keep any labels, receipts or cards of authenticity, to provide proof of the provenance. Fakes can be convincing but are not worth anything in comparison with the real thing.

BERETS AND BUCKET HATS

You have to wear a beret in Paris, *n'est-ce pas*? I have berets in yellow and red – red looks good against black and brown hair, I think. Cream looks wonderful on blondes. A redhead always suits green, it's a law of nature. I have a very sweet beret with pom-poms on top, but you have to be careful not to look like you've just been let out of kindergarten.

Bucket hats were my absolute vibe for ages, until Brooklyn Clark, the movie actress, started to call me Bucket Hat instead of my actual name. That made me wonder if I should roll back a little on them.

Hats are cute and suit everyone. In the summer, go for classic straw hats, huge and floppy or tiny and chic in muted colors. You can also get mileage from a cap.

> *I have a very sweet beret with pom-poms on top, but you have to be careful not to look like you've just been let out of kindergarten.*

Of course, you can't go out in just boots, a belt, a purse and a beret (though that sounds like the kind of ad campaign that Antoine Lambert would be very much in favor of). These accessories are the icing on the cake, but you also need a cake.

Here are my handy tips for the perfect cake. I mean, outfit.

PARIS
x

METRO

COLOUR, CONTRAST & CLASHING

COLOR

I love color! I'm a fair-skinned brunette and I suit strong colors. When I arrived from Chicago, I liked to play around with turquoise blue, bubblegum purple, neon pink and red. As I grew in confidence and absorbed a little more of that Parisian refinement, I began experimenting with pastels, and started to play around with violet, pale pink, yellow and chartreuse (a gorgeous yellow-green color named after a French liqueur, *très chic*).

If I wear paler colors, I wear more interesting prints, generally, or add a surprise element with something transparent, like a raincoat or boots. But really, anything goes. As long as it's bold in color or character, I'll wear it.

I do, of course, wear black and white – always striking and dramatic. That's sometimes enough on its own, but if I'm wearing something like my fabulous check suit with a long jacket and cute shorts, I'll add a splash of color, like my red beret.

COLOR HINTS

Add an accent of bright pink to a red outfit – like a pink bag or scarf – it's a super sophisticated combo.

Choose a vintage shade for a coat or jacket. If you want something green, go mint green, or royal blue for blue; hit yellow hard with a pure sixties sunlight shade. You'll add an essence of style that way.

Don't be afraid of abstract multicolored prints, particularly in unexpected places. I love crazy-patterned boots. Pair them with a tight floral print for joyfully clashing notes.

Mindy's Style

Mindy, a brunette like me, looks beautiful in anything. When she's not on stage, she often sports light colors: pale pink, baby blue, beige, camel. She loves gold and snakeskin to add texture and interest. If she wants to look dramatic, she'll wear all white, like a flowing long coat over a white suit. She'll put slinky high sandals with skinny jeans and look ridiculously hot. She rocks a color or a texture block – she once wore a snakeskin mini-coat with thigh-high snakeskin boots. Incredibly awesome.

She shows off her décolletage with strapless and off-the-shoulder tops, and a big frill around the shoulder line is *très* flattering.

But when Mindy starts performing … WOW! Watch out.

My favorite look of Mindy's was when she took to the stage in her half-girl, half-boy costume in the drag club she was working at. OMG, she rocked that look! Not your usual Dame Pipi, the toilet attendant. It was super cool and sooo sexy. Ever since then, there has been a showbiz vibe to her outfits, and she has brought Broadway to busking, with amazing theatrical looks like when she sang 'Sympathique' in front of the Fontaine Saint-Michel wearing thigh-high boots and a fabulous cape jacket. I also loved her elegant gown in silver and black when she sang with Benoît at Shangri-La and moved us all to tears. Now she dresses bolder than ever, with sparkling jewels, lamé suits, feathers and fur.

For Mindy, the world is a stage and every day is a chance to wear a costume.

CONTRAST

When I first arrived in Paris, I had a simple rule of thumb for contrast: put hard with soft. I'll show you what I mean.

I am a huge fan of the short skirt. I adore those little ruffled tiered skirts, often in ditzy floral prints, that just shout 1990s. That is my soft element. To add the hard, I'll team the skirt with an edgy bomber jacket over a crop top or shirt. A long leg and stiletto ankle boots give a grown-up feel. This look works well with shorts too. And *voilà*, you have mixed hard and soft!

Let's say you have a floaty and feminine skirt or dress. This needs a punky jacket. My favorites are biker, with zips, and bomber jackets, but you can also go for something sporty and boxy, or even utility. The dress is soft and the jacket hard. Sometimes one item can embody both things, like a heavy lace-up hiker boot in glitter patent. Put them with a black and red lumberjack shirt in soft brushed cotton. Perfect!

If you're wearing an edgy jacket, you can go flirty and frilly with your purse. I have one that has the most gorgeous silky fringe, like a beautiful lampshade, and I love to feel it against my legs as I walk.

It works the other way too: a punky skirt needs a feminine jacket. I love jackets that surprise. A hard-edged biker jacket in a pastel or a metallic is so pretty and embodies that hard/soft dichotomy.

Another great contrast is oversized with form-fitting. Put a tight or cinched dress with an oversized or boxy jacket and you instantly look modern.

Later, I started to try a different kind of contrast, what you might call a 'contrast of drama'. Take my harlequin knickerbockers. I teamed them with a tiny pink-fur-edged black jacket and a plaid cap. It was startling but dramatic and fun. And I started to play around with thematic dressing too – so I wore a pretty 1950s prom dress covered in hearts for our launch of the Chopard happy hearts bracelets. Maybe I learned a lesson or two from Mindy about costume. But if she is about fabulous, I will always be about fun ...

CLASH

Clash your colors and your fabrics for an up-to-the-minute, stylish edge to your outfit.

In fall, I always embrace that back-to-school preppy look with sporty cardigans, tweed shorts, high boots or lace-up Oxfords. I love a check or a bright houndstooth, and if I can match a bucket hat, I will (one of the few times I might not clash, actually!). But the cooler weather is a great opportunity to layer and mix more colors and textures, and create your clash. An outfit consisting of a cream polo neck, with a

I will always be about fun

chunky emerald-green, glitter-trimmed cardigan and a blue and pink shawl over that, a checked mini and high boots, has so many interesting elements that they sing together, no matter how unlikely they might appear at first.

I love to throw in the unexpected.

You can clash colors when they're very close in the spectrum. Blue and green work because they have similar intensity. You can do the same with any color, and if you do it with enough confidence (not like you've just forgotten to put your contact lenses in), then you'll convey exuberant sophistication.

So don't be afraid to clash: colors, fabrics and even styles. Flowing Pucci prints in purple and black swirls look amazing with a vintage Versace skirt in silk pleats. It creates magnificent discord, and showcases a clash of cultures.

Play around and find out what you like!

EVENING & PARTIES

I love to dress up for the evening. Of course, what you choose depends on what you're doing. I wear something completely different for a night out with Mindy than I would for the ballet. But wherever you're going, luxurious texture suits the evening: netting, chiffon, silk and of course velvet.

Parties are when I wear straight black, it's so very chic. I'll add interest with a character purse instead. I love a party dress with a flared skirt and a sweetheart neckline, like a fifties prom dress. I'll add vintage silver heels or classic stilettos for glamour.

Sparkle, sequins, glitter and lamé are winners for the evening. My pink silk baseball jacket over a soft pink net dress that I wore at the 'dinner' (more like a full-on house) party Mindy threw me at the Dupont house, where she worked as a nanny before getting fired, made me feel like a Pink Lady in *Grease*. But my real movie-star moment came when I went to the Opéra with a semiotics professor, Thomas, feeling like Audrey Hepburn in a beautiful, swirling black off-the-shoulder evening dress, with black gloves, a feathery black bolero jacket and a diamond necklace worn over tightly pulled-back hair. I was climbing those wonderful stairs at the Palais Garnier feeling like a star!

If I hadn't just dumped my boyfriend Doug in Chicago, and been on my way to being called a basic bitch (again) by Pierre Cadault (more about him later), it would have been perfect…

You know how I mentioned getting braver in my choice of outfits as my confidence grew? Well, when I went to Saint-Tropez, I put a purple sequinned cocktail dress in my luggage, and I'm glad I did, as Camille and I ended up at the super glam Ragazzi House (I mean, check it out, it is amazing – I have never seen a sax player floating ten feet above a swimming pool before or since!), where color and fun was so much more appropriate than plain elegance. Sparkle will never let you down.

My most princess moment was probably when I swirled in dramatic and sexy pleated red netting for Cadault's fashion show at Versailles. Now *that's* what a girl comes to Paris for!

ACCESSORIES

Scarves are a brilliant accessory, perfect for adding a shot of color or using a muted floral to soften something industrial. Camille taught me to wear them around my neck with the knot at the side in the French way.

These days I also love a headscarf. Think classic sixties look: smooth silk Hermès scarf with Prada shades. It can double as a headband too.

My favorite new accessories are gloves. I have fallen in love with fingerless leather driving gloves with stud fastenings on the back. I get them from Seymoure and they come in such wonderful colors that they look jazzy and youthful. Try taxi yellow or hot pink, and you'll see exactly what I mean.

These days I also love a headscarf

Camille's Style

Camille is a classic Parisian girl. Her style is understated, refined and chic, a little more conservative than mine, although I like to think a little of my love of the dramatic may have rubbed off on her. She is a gorgeous blonde, and in color terms, she favors navy blues and bottle greens and is often subtle in black or white. She likes to pair a sweet puff-sleeved minidress with chunky black patent loafers, and makes double denim look amazing.

If you're not a fan of vibrant color, you can take a leaf from her book and work with neutrals and classic creams and monochromes. She once wore a black and white military-style Balmain jacket at Savoir that was the *dernier cri* (last word) in Parisian fabulousness.

FINISHING TOUCHES: HAIR, JEWELRY & MAKE-UP

The finishing touches are so important. They provide polish and completion. Your clothes could look a million dollars but if you're washed-out and unadorned, the effect will be spoiled.

I keep my hair long with a center parting, and styled in soft waves, generally a little tousled, but smoother for the evening. Long and loose is my signature look and it works with just about everything. If I'm going somewhere very glamorous, I will do the full up-do and go for a smooth chignon with a hint of lift at the top, or create a textured feel with braids that are wound up to create an intricate and sophisticated style. When you're somewhere like the Galerie des Glaces at Versailles (that's the Hall of Mirrors, not the gallery of ice cream *#fauxamis*), that is the time to go for it. I dressed my hair with jewels – rhinestone pins and sprays – so that it looked as opulent as our surroundings.

I keep my jewelry simple, and wear delicate chains, layered filigree rings and simple charms. I love a choker, such as the one with little stars on a gold chain, and have even been known to wear just a ribbon tied around my neck.

Vintage jewelry is so much fun to buy and wear and it's such a thrill to find something like vintage Chanel. I was so excited the day I found my little diamond studs in the shape of entwined Cs. Chanel always adds chic. Maybe that's my motto.

You can use jewelry to stick to my hard/soft rule. I once put a Chanel chain-and-pearl necklace with a classic black leather biker jacket, and it was one of my favorite looks.

Mostly I avoid statement jewelry because my clothes are making the statement.

With make-up, I'm the same. I don't wear a lot of it, going simple with a pink or light-red lip, and some mascara. I favor a minimal, barely-there look, preferably using my favorite Durée cosmetics, which are made with macadamia nut and jojoba oils so they're nourishing too. In the evening I'll wear a stronger red lip and maybe a swoop of liquid eyeliner for a Hepburn vibe, and I do love strong brows. Mindy loves lashes. Camille favors the elaborate hair and very simple face. For nails, I go pale and pastel, but that's just me.

Sylvie is the quintessential Parisian woman, the kind who goes to bed in her eye make-up on purpose in order to look slept-in-sexy the next day.

(Ladies, I cannot recommend this. I take my make-up off religiously every night, wash, tone and moisturize, and so should you if you want to look after your skin. The only time I haven't done it is when I'm in bed but not sleeping. Then I get my make-up kissed off, rubbed off and licked off. ☺ (*#butdontforgettocleanse #Imeanit*) Everyone has to choose what makes them feel gorgeous. As I said to Sylvie once:

'You do you, and I'll do me.'
She said, 'Be you, but less.'

Which seemed to miss the point.

Sylvie's Style

The first time I met Sylvie, she was wearing her favorite color: black. A black halterneck jumpsuit with heels, subtle gold jewelry and disheveled waves in her hair. Very chic. From then on, it was a black dress, or black pants and a sleeveless top (Sylvie loves bare arms)… you get the picture.

Don't get me wrong, she looks great. She has that sexy, slouchy *je ne sais quoi* that looks effortless. She favors her hair in loose waves, although a bit more just-got-out-of-bed than mine, and she wears chunky gold earrings, a statement ring and bold cuffs.

In the evening, it's hard to get Sylvie out of black. Even her bikini is black. But she is still hard to please. Even when I wore all black, she told me it was off-black. Did you even know there was such a thing? I didn't.

Sometimes she'll concede to bottle green but always veers toward her favorite off-the-shoulder, split-to-thigh, body-hugging dresses in jersey.

I realized Sylvie was lightening up a little when she came to work one day in a gray dress. Gray! It was like she'd come adorned in rainbows. It was a neat suit in soft suede with a crossover peplum jacket over a narrow knee-length skirt, and she wore strappy high-heeled shoe-boots. See what an impression it made on me?

Sylvie goes for patterns that are non-patterns, like snakeskin. She's exactly the kind of Frenchwoman who wears a classic trench coat, preferably draped over her shoulders. *Très, très française.*

The first time she wore red – a McQueen shift dress – was the day after Pierre Cadault first called me a basic bitch. She was furious at me, of course, but I think it also cheered her up so much to see me humiliated, she decided to wear the color of victory.

DRESS
YOUR SKIN

I spend so much time thinking about visuals that I sometimes forget about the extraordinary power of fragrance.

In Paris, I learned to wear perfume, thanks to the fact that Savoir represents Maison Lavaux, the perfume house of Antoine Lambert. He was introduced to me as the best nose in France, and when I told him I thought it was very symmetrical, I discovered it actually means he designs perfumes. It's a highly respected art in France; as Antoine himself says, 'Composing a scent is like writing a symphony.'

France is the home of so many famous perfume houses, like Guerlain, Fragonard, Annick Goutal and Diptyque. All the great couture and cosmetic houses have their own scents too. Chanel has No. 5, of course, along with many others. Hermès, Dior, Saint Laurent and Lancôme are also famous for their perfumes.

Maison Lavaux designed De l'Heure which Antoine told me smelled like expensive sex. Every great scent has a bitter note, apparently, which makes it smell adult. The structure is the complex arrangement of scent molecules that create the PERFECT perfume. The perfume will have top notes, a heart, and base notes. De l'Heure has a fruitiness in its top notes, with bergamot, mandarin and vetiver. Its heart is floral, with ylang-ylang and Provençale lavender. The base note is indole. I was shocked when Antoine told us that indole has the same molecular structure as *merde* but, as my sweet colleague Luc said, in life you have to balance the sweet with the stinky. It's a weird kind of adage, but I'll take it. Now you know about the different layers in a perfume, you can have fun trying out different scents in the stores and identifying the elements. Let me know what you think of De l'Heure!

All the great couture and cosmetic houses have their own scents too. Chanel has No.5, of course, along with many others.

RULES FOR WEARING PERFUME

- **Spray on your pulse points.**

- **Never rub!** It destroys the structure of the scent! Antoine would *kill* you if he knew you'd treated his work so carelessly.

- **Allow it to develop for a while on the warmth of your skin.** Then you'll get the real spirit of the scent.

- **Not every perfume will suit you!** It all depends on your own chemical make-up how the perfume will change and develop on your individual skin. So find what smells good on you. Now you can go to Laboratoire Lavaux and try out all the fragrances and mix your own bespoke scent. Haute couture for your skin . . .

- **You can express your character through your perfume:** citrus for happy and sunny, jasmine and vanilla for flirtatious, and sandalwood and amber for depth and sexiness.

- **I never had a signature scent before I came to Paris** – in fact, I didn't really wear perfume at all – but now I think you should have several. Choose a different perfume for day and night, for the different seasons, and for your changing mood.

rfumerie sur mesure

oire lavaux

NE PONT-NEUF
LA MONNAIE
PARIS

Haute parfumerie sur mesure

laboratoire lavaux

SAMARITAINE PONT-NEUF
9 RUE DE LA MONNAIE
75001 PARIS

www.laboratoirelavaux.com

nerie sur mesure

oire lavaux

RITAINE PONT-NEUF
RUE DE LA MONNAIE
75001 PARIS

www.laboratoirelavaux.com

UNDERWEAR

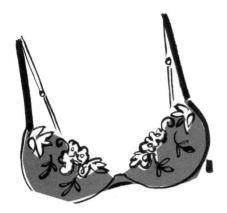

Well, what can I say? La Perla, every time. In France, men consider giving women underwear to be a liberating gesture. I can't say that completely chimes with my American outlook but you've got to admire the chutzpah. 'I'm giving you this sexy lingerie to make you a bold and confident woman and the fact I want to see you in it is just a completely unrelated aspect!' Sure … 😉

But I have to admit, beautiful underwear does make a girl feel very good. And if you can't afford La Perla, there are lots of pretty options in Paris's department stores. See my shopping guide for more.

If you don't want to wear lace, then follow Brooklyn Clark's example and wear a simple black bra and matching briefs. You can't go wrong with that.

Don't forget that if you run, like I do, you need a good supportive sports bra to protect all the delicate tissues.

I guess this guide has been all about me, and the key to fashion is that it's individual. It's all about expressing yourself and your unique character. There is no wrong way or right way, just be you. I bet you have everything you need in your closet right now to make a wonderful, bold, eclectic, playful outfit. Remember to mix the unexpected, clash colors, and contrast textures. Layer some interesting fabrics. Add a hat and a purse and the highest heels you've got.

Et voilà! Now you can walk across the Pont Neuf, take a seat at a café and sip a *café crème*, and you'll fit right in.

Et voilà! Now you can walk across the Pont Neuf, take a seat at a café and sip a café crème, and you'll fit right in.

#YouinParis

EMILY'S ROMANTIC PARIS

Chapter 2

Paris is the most romantic city in the world, of course. Everyone knows that. As I told Doug when he unaccountably did not want to join me in Paris: this city is filled with love and romance and light and beauty and passion and sex.

And it is. The moment my taxi drove down the Rue de Rivoli and past all the beautiful landmarks I'd only seen in movies, my heart was filled with it. There is just nowhere as romantic as Paris! By day or night, in all seasons.

There's even something special about being caught in an unforeseen downpour. Gabriel told me that *coup de foudre*, sudden lightning, also means love at first sight. How magical is that? It makes storms seem romantic too.

That's Paris for you.

#cityoflove

LOVE IS 'COMPLIQUÉ' (ESPECIALLY IN FRANCE)

Sylvie says, 'Sometimes the best relationships are complicated,' and she's right.

Personally, I think French people make it needlessly confusing by not wearing wedding rings like we do in America. Things would be a lot clearer if they did. Here in France, the relationships between men and women are not what I was used to at home. Of course, I knew about dating and making out and girlfriends and boyfriends. I even thought I knew about love. Doug and I were in love, we had sex, we spent lots of time together and he listened to me most of the time. I thought I was grown up. But when I got to Paris, I didn't feel grown up at all. In fact, I felt all kinds of gauche.

Here, people are both super aware of sex and super unaware of boundaries. That makes everything that happens feel very loaded. The very first man I met in Paris kissed me on both cheeks, flirted and asked me out for a drink, all in the space of five minutes. Before I even knew his name.

When I told him I had a boyfriend, he said in so many words that if my boyfriend wasn't in Paris, it didn't count. Maybe that was my first hint that things in this city weren't going to be exactly straightforward.

My next clue was when a married man – and a client – started coming on to me in front of his wife. And, I later discovered, in front of his mistress. And *that*, apparently, was not the done thing at all. As you'll have probably worked out, that was Antoine, and the mistress was Sylvie.

But these complicated relationships are not considered so strange here in Paris. In fact, as long as there are no nasty secrets, people seem to be at ease with infidelity.

Mindy's Wisdom

A man should never flirt
with another woman in front
of his mistress

After all, Sylvie and her husband (Laurent, from Laurent G fame) live separate lives with separate lovers, and both are happy with that. In fact, you know what? I think they're still in love, and maybe it's because they are free to choose that.

The French seem very comfortable with the idea of lovers. My first conversation with Thomas, the semiotics professor, was a speculation about the exact relationship between the older woman and younger man sitting in front of us at the café. Of course, he thought they were lovers. It's the default setting here.

French men are very keen to make women feel attractive. Even in normal life, people say '*enchanté*' instead of 'how do you do.' I mean – enchanted! You have to admit that's endearing. So much more romantic than saying 'How ya doing?' or 'Nice to meet you.' I love the idea that people are enchanted to meet me, especially as I'm usually very enchanted indeed to meet them. If you mix the murmured *enchanté* with the hand-kissing and meaningful stare, it all becomes somewhat overwhelming…

In my experience, most Frenchmen will try to push their luck. They like flirtation and assume you'll be flattered that they hit on you.

But it's not all sweetness and light. All this enchantment can hide creeps, like the guy at that party at the Dupont house. He was frankly vulgar. It can conceal snobs, like Thomas, whose charm and sexiness disappeared when he turned out to look down on everyone, but particularly me. (Warning: the French take your culture quotient *very* seriously. You need to know your Duras from your Dumas, your Monet from your Manet and your Bizet from your Berlioz. Apparently if you can distinguish Dior from Givenchy and YSL from LV, it doesn't really count … at least, not to intellectuals.) Never trust a man who can't make love to you unless he's vetted your bookcase first. *#prioritiesandpaperbacks*

In my experience, most Frenchmen will try to push their luck. They comment on your looks, your lashes, your legs. They like flirtation and assume you'll be flattered that they hit on you. They think it's a compliment, where we might think it's harassment. It's a different point of view and I sometimes have a problem getting my head around it.

I have to admit it often seems kind of reductive and sexist to me. But French women seem to cope. Sylvie said she is not a feminist, and yet she is one of the most kick-ass women I know, who won't take shit from anyone. She certainly thinks she's as good as any man. In fact, most French women know they're better, but to keep men happy, act as if they aren't. It's not the American way, let's be honest.

The great thing is that most men are not offended if you say no politely. They shrug, smile and everyone is still friends. I still think you need to keep your boundaries. So don't be afraid to say *non, merci*, no matter how much La Perla lingerie they give you.

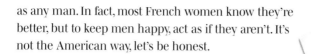

Mindy's Wisdom

The French are romantic but they are also realists

THINGS THAT WILL HAPPEN A LOT IN PARIS

KISSING

Everyone kisses very enthusiastically all the time. You will get a kiss on each cheek from someone you've literally just laid eyes on. And every now and then, like when I met Camille, you meet in the middle by mistake and get a smooch full on the lips. I wonder if the French designed the two-kiss system especially for that purpose. It would not surprise me. *#anyexcuse*

And of course you'll see lovers kissing – on bridges, in squares, in the parks, in the street... Soon you won't be able to help yourself. If you can't beat them... 😘*#akissisjustakiss*

NUDITY

Paris is the first place where I saw a fully naked woman walking around in the open air. And no one else seemed to turn a hair. Okay, it was the ad campaign for Maison Lavaux, but it made me realize that the French are a lot more at ease with nudity than we are in the States. In Champagne, I had to deal with Gérard, Camille's father, baring everything by the pool, and at the hammam spa where Camille took me for a sauna, all the girls had their boobs out but me. It just felt too awkward. I guess I am a modest American girl at heart and it might be a while before I can go full Parisian naked in public. *#barelythere*

FLIRTATION

It's in the eyes. From everyone. All the time. Men, women, bosses, co-workers. No one seems to be afraid of harassment suits, or even that other people will think it's inappropriate. If anything, half the time I expect to be told off for not being flirtatious enough. Antoine not only sent me that lingerie, he also sent Sylvie nipple rings, for goodness' sake! Surely a tad inappropriate, even for Paris! Mathieu, Pierre Cadault's nephew who dumped me as the train left the platform of the Gare de Lyon, flirted with me as soon as we met. My realtor flirted, my Champagne tour guide flirted (ahem, yes, you know how that ended)... you get the picture.

The only straight man who didn't flirt right away was Alfie. Maybe because he's British. *#stiffupperlip* Even he loosened up in the end... *#theBritishunbuttoned*

#akissisjustakiss

Mindy's Wisdom

French men never get tired of
having sex. It's like docking
them in a lightning port

SEX

Everything in Paris is about sex. The whole city seems to exist almost entirely so
people can get laid. The restaurants, the hotels, the bars, the clubs, the galleries, the
parks, the beautiful riverside … all of it appears designed to encourage people to
make love as soon as they get the next possible opportunity. Even the champagne
coupes are preferred to flutes because they are more sexy and modeled on Marie
Antoinette's breasts. Tell me they are not obsessed. Please.

The sex should also be *coquin* – naughty (Sylvie's word). When I suggested that a
signature scent and a hotel could be like the perfect marriage, Antoine immediately
jumped in and said, 'Let's call it an affair – much more romantic,' as hotels are mostly
used for illicit liaisons. That's the theory, true or not. Personally, I don't believe every
tourist in Paris is having an affair, but you can't deny that some hotels are perfect for
a sexy tryst, with a bar, a bedroom and a bathroom in dangerously close proximity.

The French are unabashed about their belief in sex as the answer to most things.
Mathieu told me that when things were at their darkest during World War Two, the
French made love. I thought maybe planning a defensive strategy might have been
more use, but I guess they needed those endorphins. After all, Sylvie thinks that
if you're feeling tense, sex is one of the best ways to relax. A little bit like Brooklyn
Clark, who told me she has to masturbate after a long flight (maybe they're more
alike than I realized?).

Sex can be pretty poetic here. After all, they call an orgasm *la petite mort*, which
means 'a little death'. That sounds so romantic, if slightly macabre. Better than
orgasm though, which has a distinctly medical ring.

Poetry takes precedence in Paris. Thomas quoted me the Frenchpoet Rimbaud
during sex. SOOO French. And a tad pretentious.
#dontpretendyouwerentthinkingthesamething

Thomas also didn't shower after sex, which surprised me, but Mindy says it's typically
French. I can't even tell you what she says the *métro* smells of in rush hour, but it
made me want a shower right then and there.

Mindy's Wisdom

♡ You haven't done Paris right until you've had at least one wildly inappropriate affair!

My own experience of sex here has been pretty good. Even when I slept with Timothée, who turned out to be just out of high school (so 'petite-mortifying'), he was gentle and sweet, if a little overenthusiastic. I guess he was a beginner. Louise, his mother, called me to her office to tackle the very serious matter of whether he was a good lover or not. *#Frenchmama #maternalpriorities*

Thomas was wonderful as long as we didn't do too much talking. *Petites morts* and poetry don't always go together.

Alfie and I had fun. I really enjoyed hooking up in his apartment in La Défense. *#defensesdown*

But Gabriel … well, I didn't know it could be like that. Suddenly, I understood what it could be, what it was all for, and why everyone in Paris is obsessed with it. It was amazing, life-changing, an orchestra playing a symphony in my body, it was … *ooh là là!*

Maybe that's why I don't want to leave Paris.

ROMANTIC HOTELS FOR A SEXY PARIS TRYST

- **Hôtel Plaza Athénée**
  This gorgeous hotel is on the Avenue Montaigne in the
  heart of haute couture. This was where Brooklyn Clark
  not only nearly lost Savoir 2 million euros, but where
  she partied so hard that my picture of her Pierre
  Cadault dress went viral. Definitely a place for losing your head in bed.

- **Hôtel de Crillon**
  One of the grandest old hotels in Paris, this Beaux Arts landmark has stunning
  views of the Place de la Concorde, scene of the annual Bastille Day celebrations
  on July 14th. Its luxurious rooms are perfect for a delicious honeymoon or a very
  coquin weekend.

- **Hôtel Le Meurice**
  Known for a while as the hotel of kings due to all its royal visitors, this classic hotel
  was the first in Paris to provide a bathroom for each room – a must for any really
  sexy tryst. It's been a favorite of artists including Dalí, Picasso and Warhol, and
  looks out on the Rue de Rivoli, one of Paris's premier shopping streets, with views
  of the Tuileries Garden.

- **The Ritz**
  Iconic and illustrious, the Ritz boasts a pedigree of distinction. A favorite of
  royalty, models, writers, artists, and, of course, designers. Coco Chanel lived here
  for years, just around the corner from her *atelier* (designer workshop). If you want
  true old-style glamour with a helping of fashion, the Ritz is the one for you.

- **Zimmer Paris**
  Super stylish and full of wonderful modern art, this hotel is Savoir's client
  Randy Zimmer's latest outpost. With amazing food and a sexy vibe, its unique
  aphrodisiac quality is provided by its signature scent (the one for affairs),
  designed exclusively for Zimmer by Maison Lavaux. It will drive you and your
  lover wild!

PLACES TO BREAK UP

Paris is a veritable treasure trove of perfect settings. Here are just a few of mine, but you'll find so many more of your own. Life and love are full of ups and downs, but Paris has a place for every occasion.

THE PANTHÉON

Be like me and break up long distance in front of the Panthéon. Maybe it's the fact that it's a mausoleum – symbolic of the death of my relationship with Doug – that made it so appropriate. It does add a certain grandeur as a backdrop, with its magnificent columns, classical pediment and the tricolore flying at the top. And it's a reminder that all things must pass, including a horrible transatlantic dumping.

THE STEPS OF THE PALAIS GARNIER

If someone calls you simple-minded and you want to make the best exit ever, then walking away up the magnificent marble stairs of the Opéra Garnier is the perfect way to do it. The opera house, which also hosts the ballet, is renowned for its opulent Napoleon III baroque style, and the marble staircase is decorated with *torchères*, statues of women holding huge lampstands boasting dozens of glittering bulbs. This place is famous as the setting of *The Phantom of the Opera*, and is drop-dead glamorous. So why not showcase your break-up by doing it practically on a stage?

THE GARE DE LYON

This is where Mathieu Cadault and I were leaving for that romantic weekend in Saint-Tropez. We were aboard our luxurious train and about to speed to the south when he heard me talking to Gabriel on the phone, and broke up with me on the spot. I mean, the train was actually moving and he still managed to get off with his luggage, to avoid being with me. But a station or an airport is actually a classic place for a break-up – think *Brief Encounter* or *Casablanca*. Everyone around you is too busy to take much notice of the drama and you can easily make a quick getaway on whatever mode of transport is handy.

SACRÉ COEUR

For a *Moulin Rouge* vibe, head to Montmartre, the traditional home of poverty-stricken artists including Toulouse Lautrec. At the highest point stands the Basilique du Sacré Coeur, the Sacred Heart. With all of Paris glittering below, you'll feel the full

force of a tragic broken heart. There's a whole
magnificent monument dedicated to a bleeding heart
right behind you. Very apt.

BRASSERIE LA COUPOLE

This is where Alfie and I had our last rendezvous
before he told me he was returning to London. I
don't know if it qualifies as a break-up or not – yet.
But I felt it was an improvement on being dropped
over the phone while on the street. La Coupole is a
famous brasserie in Montparnasse, built in the roaring
twenties. Its art-deco style with accents of mint green
and black helped to soothe my confusion over what
to do next. Was it all over for Alfie and me? The great
thing about being in a chic restaurant is that you both
have to behave well. No shouting allowed.

PLACES
TO MAKE UP
(OR MAKE OUT)

THE TOP OF THE EIFFEL TOWER

Why not? It can be a little windy but the views are amazing. See all of Paris laid
out around you, and be moved by the iconic beauty of an amazing edifice. Created by
Gustave Eiffel for the World Fair of 1889, it's over 1,000 feet high and is now a national
monument and symbol of Paris. I just have to try and forget Luc and Julien showing me
the Eiffel Tower sex position ... oh, sorry, try to wipe that from your mind and concentrate
on the romance. If you don't like heights, you can always make up underneath it.

THE BATEAUX MOUCHES

Or, as I said to Sylvie, the bateaux smooch. Even Alfie, with all his British cynicism,
couldn't resist falling in love with Paris from the deck of the bateau mouche, the
boat that cruises up and down the Seine, giving you the most amazing view of the
city. I guess it helped that I was wearing that heart dress and we were celebrating
Chopard's happy hearts bracelets (subliminal message, much?). He'd said that Paris
was just a scam, a made-up marketing ploy like any other, and I had fallen for it. But
watching the Eiffel Tower sparkling above us, Alfie had to give in and concede that
Paris is all about romance, if you let it work its magic. #surrenderoftheBritish

The bateaux mouches travel up and down the river all day and into the night.
You can see the lights of Paris in a totally new way, as you drift past Notre-Dame,
the Musée d'Orsay, the Eiffel Tower and all the other iconic
sites of the city. Go at sunset and watch the reflections
begin to shimmer on the water as night falls. The city
looks like an electric rainbow.

*The bateaux smooch!
Go at sunset and watch
the reflections begin to
shimmer on the water as
night falls.*

RUE DE L'ABREUVOIR – THE ROAD THAT GOES TO THE END

On my first visit here with Mindy, I thought I was breaking up – breaking up with my Instagram account on Sylvie's instructions. But the next day, I was snuggling up to Camille in a Hästens bed on the prettiest street in Paris for the campaign for our Swedish client, and my Insta was safe and well after all. What a relief! You'll find this gorgeous place in Montmartre. It looks idyllic with cobblestones, lampposts and the prettiest of buildings lining its gentle slope. If that's not a wonderful place to make up, what is? If you can bring your own bed, so much the better. Gabriel loves sleeping under the stars. Not that it matters.

L'ATELIER DES LUMIÈRES

This amazing place is where you can step inside the works of famous artists. The paintings are enlarged, lit and projected, and made to move. The liquid beauty is truly something else, and you can lose yourself from top to toe in the romance of art. Be transported to Van Gogh's *Starry Night* in Saint-Rémy-de-Provence, and you will feel utterly full of beauty, your heart will expand, and you will not be able to help falling in love with the person you are next to. I know. I was sitting next to Gabriel.

CANAL SAINT-MARTIN AND THE SEINE

Who can resist walking hand in hand along the Canal Saint-Martin or by the river, under the strings of lights, stopping only to order a glass of wine at one of the outdoor tables of a café or bistro? Parisians love to take a stroll by the water. If you go to the canal, which connects the river to a larger canal to the north, you'll follow the romantic route we walked as a foursome: Gabriel, Camille, Thomas and me. No one can deny that walking alongside the glittering water is truly seductive.

PLACE DES VOSGES

Le Marais is one of my favorite parts of Paris: chic, quirky, stylish and individual. It is historic and yet modern at the same time and bursting with adorable romantic bistros and pretty streets. The Place des Vosges is the old square in the heart of Le Marais, surrounded by stunning cloisters that have shops and galleries to explore. In the center is a beautiful garden with a fountain. In the summer, bring your lover, a picnic and a bottle of champagne, and prepare to lie on the grass and kiss – or do what Mindy does and kiss Benoît with falafel breath.

L'APPARTEMENT

It turned out that Mathieu Cadault used a visit to his amazing apartment as his 'go-to move', but I had to admit, it was impressive and the view itself was enough to make you fall into bed at once, overcome by desire. At Alfie's apartment in La Défense, a business district a few miles out of the city, I discovered a side of sleek and sophisticated urban living that I hadn't yet seen. No wonder I felt at home in his pinstriped business jacket the next morning, in a place that is part home, part office. I was glad to be back on familiar ground though.

I know that Sylvie's super chic apartment in Saint-Germain-des-Prés (a very elegant district of Paris) has been the scene of many a seduction.

But my favorite place for that has to be my own *chambre de bonne*, on the fifth floor, with its romantic view of the cobbled square below, the lampposts and the fountain. I've had quite a few *petites morts* in my little flat, though I have to admit that's all a lot easier to arrange when Mindy isn't my roommate. The *ménage à trois* (threesome) is one aspect of French tradition I haven't really wanted to experience, and Mindy is adamant about her feelings on the subject. Like her, I prefer one in one. I mean, one on one.

Place des Vosges

A BRIDGE
TO ROMANCE

You're probably wondering why I haven't mentioned the most romantic places of all in Paris: the bridges. After all, I adore them. But that's because I think that this aspect of this incredible city deserves a whole category of its own.

You can't go to Paris and not be wowed by the bridges. The city is split in two halves, the Left Bank and Right Bank, by the curving Seine that makes its stately way across it. Over the river there are thirty-seven bridges. Bridges are not only romantic in themselves, they also offer fantastic opportunities for very gorgeous Insta content. Here are my favorites.

PONT ALEXANDRE III

Named after Tsar Alexander III of Russia, this bridge is known as the most beautiful bridge in the world! It's like something out of a musical, a magnificent construction of white stone, with a pair of gilt bronze statues of winged horses at each end and amazing lamps along its length. There are sweeping views of the Grand Palais, the Petit Palais and other iconic landmarks. On this bridge, we shot that ad campaign for De l'Heure with that beautiful naked model walking across it. The whole thing was closed just for us, which felt very special although I wasn't especially comfortable with the concept.

PONT DES ARTS – OR THE LOVERS' LOCKS BRIDGE

You might have heard of the quaint tradition of lovers in Paris writing their names on a padlock, locking it to a bridge and tossing the key into the Seine to signify their unbreakable bond. This was the bridge where hundreds and hundreds of padlocks were locked into place. It was a good idea in the beginning, but soon there were so many, the structure of the bridge was compromised by the weight, and they were all removed. The bridge was reconstructed with iron and glass so that the locks couldn't be reattached.

I love this sweet footbridge and come here all the time to watch darkness descend and the lights of Paris begin to sparkle. Very talented buskers sometimes sing here in the daytime.

By the way, it's now a criminal offense to put padlocks around Paris, so maybe think of some other way to celebrate your unbreakable bond. After all, an Instagram post lasts forever! Unless you delete it.

Bridges are great for Insta content

Pont Neuf

PONT NEUF

In typically confusing French style, the name means the New Bridge, so naturally it is the oldest surviving bridge in Paris, constructed in 1578. I suppose it was new then, and as it was the first, I guess it made sense. I mean, it's not like they thought that in five hundred years it would no longer be new but old, so they should call their brand-new bridge the Old Bridge.

It was ordered to be built by King Henri IV and connects the Rue de Rivoli to Rue Dauphine. You must walk across this bridge, if only to ponder the whole old/new thing, but of course it's stunning as well and an amazing piece of history.

PONT DE LA TOURNELLE

This bridge is one of my favorites for a run, taking me over from the Left Bank to the Île Saint-Louis, where I can stop for a Berthillon ice cream at Le Flore en l'Île. This beautiful old bridge gives an amazing view of Notre-Dame and the statue of her patron saint Sainte Geneviève, who apparently encouraged early Parisians to resist the hordes of Attila the Hun and hold firm to save the city. Her statue is protectively holding a child, who represents Paris.

PONT SAINT-MICHEL

This bridge has been reconstructed several times since it first linked the Left and Right Banks at the Place Saint-Michel and the Île de la Cité, and it was most recently rebuilt in 1857. I like it because I first saw it when Mathieu took me for a ride in his beautiful motorboat and we whizzed under the arches. Above them, on the side of the bridge, are large carved stone Ns for Napoleon, each one surrounded in a carved laurel wreath. They are so elegant and made a beautiful post for my Insta.

You can't go to Paris and not be wowed by the bridges.

The truth is that no matter what I say you will find romantic spots all over the city, and I just hope you have the perfect person to share them with.

Finding that person is the hard part, and harder still if you're living by the confusing rules of a different culture. If I'd known a little bit more about how the French think, maybe I would have been more honest with Camille about my feelings for Gabriel, and told her what had happened between us from the start.

But I got so confused about what was going on, and I found the attraction to Gabriel so overwhelming I wasn't able to control myself. I'm not sure if I should never have slept with him, or if I should have told Camille the truth and let things fall as they may. After all, we promised that neither of us would get involved. And Camille didn't stick to that promise, even though I did.

I still don't know what to do about it.

Sylvie's Wisdom

♡ While you're here, fall in love, make mistakes, leave a disastrous trail in your wake

I respect Sylvie a lot. I think she knows about life. So watch this space …

MUSIC TO FALL IN LOVE BY IN PARIS

'*La Vie en Rose*' – Édith Piaf

'*Sympathique*' – Mindy Chen

'*Sous le Ciel de Paris*' – Juliette Greco

'*La Mer*' – Charles Trenet

'*Plus Je T'embrasse*' – Blossom Dearie

'*Non, Je Ne Regrette Rien*' – Édith Piaf

'*Ne Me Quitte Pas*' – Jacques Brel

'*Tous les Garçons et les Filles*' – Françoise Hardy

'*Je Ne Te Quitte Pas*' – Fred Nevché

'*Chez Keith et Anita*' – Carla Bruni

'*Je Cherche un Homme*' – Eartha Kitt

EMILY'S SHOPPING PARIS

Chapter 3

'J'aime beaucoup faire du shopping!'

That is my way of saying that I like to shop very much (I think it's correct French but I can't be absolutely sure. I really try to concentrate in my French classes but it isn't always easy, especially if a handsome and moody British guy is sitting at the next table).

I don't think it will come as a great surprise to anyone that I like shopping. Like is too mild. I **love** shopping. LOVE IT.

I LOVE SHOPPING!!!

#shoppingismylife

When I was growing up, I loved *The Devil Wears Prada*. When fashion assistant Andi gets to go to Paris with magazine editor Miranda at the end, I was like yaaaas, girrrl, you've made it! ✿ ✍ (And it made me yearn for my own Parisian adventure … which is partly how I ended up here.)

Then she suddenly forgets everything she's learned and throws it all away. It's heartbreaking. Andi got brainwashed into thinking that fashion is frivolous and doesn't matter, when the movie had been trying to show her the opposite all along. Fashion *does* matter. It is one of life's pleasures, like food or reading or art. Would you say food doesn't matter? That books are frivolous? That art is meh? Of course not! You might say that there's good food and bad food. I don't disagree. A Chicago deep-dish pizza might not be haute cuisine but there's a place for it, right? (I don't mean the trash can, Julien!) And a Michelin-starred meal is a work of art. With books, there's pulp fiction and there's great literature. In art, there's a so-so sketch – and Monet's *Water Lilies* or the *Mona Lisa*. At the movies you can see a summer blockbuster or a timeless art-house classic.

Clothes are just the same. There's disposable fashion and exquisite couture. Both count but in different ways. High fashion is an achievement. That's why there are fashion schools and museums – so that we can teach and preserve this art. Once you get an eye for craftmanship, there is an incredible enjoyment that comes from seeing and holding something that is perfectly made to the highest of standards. Couture is an art, and it deserves awe and respect. It's art you can wear.

I won't apologize to anyone for my love of fashion. Until you've seen a Pierre Cadault dress in the *atelier*, and examined the exquisite stitching, the expert embroidery, the fineness of the fabric, the inspired cut and construction, all thanks to the hours of work of dozens of highly skilled craftspeople (weavers, button-makers, cutters, seamstresses, trimmers, finishers …), well, until then, don't dismiss fashion just like that. Don't tell me it's a silly and vain pursuit for empty-headed people (women, mostly). It's just not true.

How do we remember an era? Mostly by its clothes. The roaring twenties? Sure, fringed dresses, feather headbands, ropes of pearls, gangster suits, two-toned shoes, homburg hats … The sexy sixties? Minidresses, white plastic boots, swirling psychedelic patterns and flower prints. Eighties? Hello, shoulder pads and power dressing! I could go on. We define ourselves through clothes. Every day we make a decision about how we will look and how we will present ourselves to the world. And clothes bring joy, expression and theater to our lives.

DEEP BREATH. Er … OMG. Did I just say all of that? I have no excuses. I'm passionate. Lecture over. And the good news is that if fashion matters, then shopping matters.

I have no excuses. I'm passionate. Lecture over. And the good news is that if fashion matters, then shopping matters.

My hobby is practically an art form!

WAYS
TO SHOP

There are so many different ways to shop, from the personal appointment at the *atelier* or the private shopper at the grand department store, through to mass-market retail, the mall and the discount store, all the way to thrift, resale and consignment stores, and, finally, the outdoor markets. And you can shop without leaving your house, thanks to the internet.

Everything has something to recommend it, and I don't think you should be a snob about any of it. You could find an amazing outfit in any thrift store for just a few dollars and look awesome, while congratulating yourself on your ecological credentials. But it takes time, imagination and creativity, and a certain fearlessness as well.

Stores remove some of that burden and curate what they offer you so that you can assemble a look from their stock. Most assistants can offer a word or two of advice if you're at a loss. Or you get ideas from your favorite movies, shows, bands or magazines, or from friends whose looks you admire, and go for a version that you think will suit you.

There are tons of ways to approach how to find the clothes you want to wear. I just know you'll find the ones that work for you.

There is nowhere like Paris for clothes shopping. Every major city in the world has its luxe district, where you'll find the famous names. But Paris has the edge because it is the birthplace and home of some of the greatest couture in the world.

After all, the term 'haute couture' itself is, of course, French, and literally means 'high sewing' or 'dressmaking' and the term is protected in law. The Chambre Syndicale de la Haute Couture, the governing body of fashion, decides which *atelier* qualifies for the term and a new list is published each year.

Let's say a fairy godmother comes with her bibbity-boppity-boo magic wand and waves it. Kapow! You have a platinum credit card without a limit. Congratulations!

Let's go shopping!

HAUTE COUTURE

To qualify as haute couture, a designer must:

- *design bespoke clothes for a customer, fitted to their measurements on site.*

- *have an 'atelier' in Paris that employs at least fifteen full-time members of staff.*

- *have at least twenty full-time artisans (the people making the clothes) in the 'atelier'.*

- *present a collection of at least fifty originally designed garments to the public twice a year (in January and July) of day and evening wear.*

A high-end designer is often known as a *couturier*. The term haute couture is now pretty loosely used to describe high fashion all over the world.

The first haute couture houses included Lanvin, Chanel, Mainbocher, Schiaparelli, Dior and Balenciaga. Later, Yves Saint Laurent, Balmain, Givenchy and Jean Paul Gaultier also joined, along with other famous names.

It is hugely expensive and prestigious to produce collections like this twice a year, or more. Most of the large fashion houses rely on diffusion lines to ensure a reach to those who cannot afford the extraordinary prices of haute couture. Most houses will offer perfumes, sunglasses, bags, make-up, shoes and jewelry, as well as ready-to-wear lines, and this brings in most of their revenue.

MY FAVORITE DESIGNERS & THEIR STORES

The premier shopping district of Paris is known as the Golden Triangle. It's in the 8th arrondissement, the heart of the most expensive part of Paris. It's bordered by the Avenue Montaigne, the Champs-Élysées and the Avenue George V. Here you will find the ultimate luxury hotels and businesses, high-end apartments and, of course, the home of haute couture. Dominated by a stunning view of the Eiffel Tower, Avenue Montaigne is stuffed with modern-day temples of fashion. Just nearby is the Rue du Faubourg Saint-Honoré, the Rue Saint-Honoré and Place Vendôme.

My favorite designers are in this exclusive district. Call into these amazing shops, be awed by the scale and luxury, and overwhelmed by the work of the present-day designers keeping the torches of fashion legend blazing. They are the stuff of dreams. When you've had enough, go to the Hôtel Plaza Athénée or the George V for a restorative orange pressée and some *viennoiseries* (pastries, yum yum).

Chanel

Chanel is a byword for style, glamour and everything chic, and is also associated with powerful women thanks to its founder Gabrielle Chanel, better known by her nickname Coco. Coco spent part of her childhood in a convent where she learned to sew, and later opened a small shop in Deauville by the sea. Here, she began to revolutionize the way women dressed, freeing them from long skirts and corsets with easy trousers, skirts and Breton stripe tops.

Chanel became famous for its innovative use of jersey, a fabric that is fluid and easy to wear. Later, the tweed suit, the little black dress, the quilted chain handbag and two-toned pumps and flats all became signatures known throughout the world. The white camellia emblem and the scent Chanel No. 5 remain totemic.

Chanel's legacy was and is carefully guarded, first by Karl Lagerfeld until his death, and now by Virginie Viard, who continues to work with the Chanel elements: tweed, quilting, pearls and camellias.

Coco Chanel

CHANEL
31 RUE CAMBON PARIS

- **FAMOUS FANS:** *Keira Knightley, Kristen Stewart, Vanessa Paradis*

- **FLAGSHIP STORE:** *31 Rue Cambon is the Chanel headquarters; in 1918, Coco Chanel purchased the first of five townhouses that would form the 'atelier' and the main store, with her apartment on the second floor, still perfectly preserved. A new flagship is 19 Rue Cambon, just across from 31. It is a gorgeous marvel of ivory, black and blonde, with accents of crystal and gold, and full of tributes to Chanel's favorite motifs: wheatsheafs, lion's heads, Chinese screens, and, of course, camellias. It is also full of glorious fashion.*

Christian Dior

Born in the early twentieth century, Dior at first wanted to be an artist but ended up learning his craft in an *atelier*. In 1946, he set up his own label and wowed the world with his New Look, which featured a wasp waist and full, petticoated skirt. With its shorter, narrow skirts and boxy jackets, it caused a sensation after years of rationing, though it also brought fierce criticism of indulgence and waste.

But Dior had put Paris back on the map as the heart of fashion and haute couture. He employed a young designer whose talent he recognized, and left control of his fashion house to him. His name was Yves Saint Laurent. Dior has continued to be a byword for ladylike elegance, with its famous Dior bag and signature scent, Miss Dior, named after Christian Dior's war heroine sister. Today Maria Grazia Chiuri carries on the Dior legend.

- **FAMOUS FANS:** *Natalie Portman, Charlize Theron, Rihanna*

- **FLAGSHIP STORE:** *Dior has just opened an incredible store at 30 Avenue Montaigne in Paris. Inside is a fantastically designed space in accents of white. A grand staircase curves up a stairwell hung with Dior creations and huge roses stretch up toward the ceiling. The 108,000-square-foot space offers a dazzling boutique, a gallery, a restaurant and a patisserie, and three gardens – a thrilling experience of luxury.*

Yves Saint Laurent

Yves Saint Laurent was only twenty-one when he found himself as the head of Dior, and is credited with saving it. Later he founded his own fashion house and was hugely influential, creating Le Smoking, a tuxedo jacket for women, and other fashion-forward modern looks. Today his *atelier* is led by Anthony Vaccarello.

- **FAMOUS FANS:** *Dua Lipa, Zoë Kravitz, Blackpink's Rosé*

- **FLAGSHIP STORE:** *Modern, marble and monochrome, the YSL flagship store on the Avenue Montaigne is a fitting setting for the forward-thinking label. Achingly chic and showcasing the new seasons in style, this wonderful store is a must-see, especially if you've just been to Dior.*

Givenchy

Hubert de Givenchy opened his fashion house in the early fifties and was an instant success. He gave us the shirt dress, the sack dress and the baby doll look. He dressed Audrey Hepburn in several of her films including, famously, *Breakfast at Tiffany's*. Givenchy is renowned for French chic and understated, elegant style and today the label is designed by Matthew M. Williams.

- **FAMOUS FANS:** *K-pop girl group Aespa, Ariana Grande, Kendall Jenner*

- **FLAGSHIP STORE:** *At 36 Avenue Montaigne, Givenchy is discreet and aristocratic, with a muted interior in dark green, black and brass, underpinned by lots of marble and wooden floors. Absolute refinement rules here, which is no surprise for a label that insists on understatement and elegance. You must come here and imagine you can see Audrey Hepburn taking a stroll among the rails to see what the new season has to offer her. Bliss!*

Pierre Cadault

Pierre Cadault is one of France's most legendary designers. He is famous for his affair with Elton John and his feud with Valentino, though that fades into insignificance next to his grand combat with Grégory Duprée, his one-time collaborator. He is a temperamental genius who has learned to love tackiness in order to stay relevant, and has a tendency to go off the rails. Luckily he has Mathieu to help keep him in check. He often wears black with a shawl over one shoulder and huge dark glasses.

- **FAMOUS FANS:** *Brooklyn Clark, Patricia Field*

- **FLAGSHIP STORE:** *Pierre Cadault's 'atelier' and private boutique are situated in a secret location just off the Avenue Montaigne. I'm afraid that it is strictly appointment only, so only a lucky few will ever get to see the master's work IRL. But you can find some of his ready-to-wear collection in the big department stores and his collaborations are some of his most popular work.*

Don't forget Celine and Chloé, smaller haute couture labels that are powerhouses of style and elegance, and completely French in their outlook.

I hope you enjoyed that tour of some of the great Parisian designers. Did you use your fairy-godmother credit? What did you spend your fairy-tale cash on? I hope you managed to get a little something that you can take home and enjoy in the real world.

Pierre Cadault
is one of France's most
legendary designers!

PARIS'S MOST FAMOUS DEPARTMENT STORES

So, let's now make our way to the wonderful French invention that has created a whole new way to shop and made a lot of people very happy at the same time. And, you might be surprised to learn, it revolutionized employment as well, giving workers paid vacation, pensions and free cafeteria lunches. The grand department store! A one-stop shop where you can find everything you needed to dress and live well. Paris has the most wonderful, iconic stores, like the Belle Époque ('beautiful age'), that are worth visiting just to see their exquisite interiors.

LE BON MARCHÉ

This wonderful store started life as a market stall, then became a shop and then, finally, in 1867, a department store. It is housed in a stunning art-deco building co-designed by Gustave Eiffel. You'll find all the major designers here but also lots of smaller labels and big consumer favorites. It offers clothes, shoes, beauty and accessories, as well as everything you could need for your home, and the food hall – La Grande Épicerie – alone is worth a visit, just to see the amazing array of delicacies from all over the world laid out in the huge and impressive space dedicated to the finest of foods and wines. Visit this Paris institution on the Left Bank and enjoy!

LA SAMARITAINE

This famous luxury department store, situated in the 1st arrondissement, started life as a small clothing shop, and fashion is still what it does best, with a cornucopia of wonderful labels. The interior has a marvelous light feel thanks to its huge glass roof surrounded by stunning art-deco tiles, with beautiful staircases leading up through the floors.

There are fabulous restaurants, and it's eco-conscious too, running on renewable energy, which makes shopping there practically guilt-free. I spent a very happy hour shopping with Petra, my neighbor from French class, and it was all going very well until she decided to walk out without paying. I don't have to tell you that even if Petra may have managed to escape with her shopping *gratuit*, shoplifting is very wrong!

GALERIES LAFAYETTE

You must see this stunning store on the Boulevard Haussmann in the 9th. The incredible dome that dominates the interior is breathtaking. It's another art-nouveau treasure full of beautiful things to buy; you'll be completely seduced by this Paris landmark. Every Friday a fashion show is presented, open to the public as long as you book in advance, which I think is a marvelous idea that more shops should offer! There are cafés, restaurants and bars, but go to the rooftop for panoramic views of Paris.

PRINTEMPS

Another Paris institution, also on the Boulevard Haussmann, is Printemps. Their slogan is 'Printemps, nous avons des vêtements!', which means 'we have clothes'. It's my homing call! Founded in the nineteenth century, this store was one of the first to offer elevators, a huge novelty. This place also has a gorgeous art nouveau dome. It was taken down piece by piece before the war in case of bombs and restored afterwards. Visit for all manner of fashion, with something for every budget.

THE PASSAGES

The passages are a very special feature of shopping in Paris. A completely charming relic of an older shopping world, these covered arcades, with their wrought iron and glass roofs, house dozens of shops, galleries and restaurants. There are around twenty passages in the area around the Grands Boulevards and up near the Opéra. Here are a few you should take a look at if you can.

– Passage des Panoramas

This is the oldest of the passages, founded in 1799, and it has a delightful old-fashioned air. You'll find books, coins, prints, chocolate, antiques, and many more unusual treasures. If you want to find antique stamps, this is your place. Pretend you're back in the nineteenth century as you wander through this fascinating place.

– Galerie Vivienne

One of the most iconic passages, situated by the Palais-Royal. With its beautiful roof and inlaid mosaic floor, it's a wonderful place to retreat from the traffic and rain to enjoy a drink at one of the cafés and watch the clouds pass by overhead. Pass the time browsing in the boutiques.

– Passage Jouffroy

One of the most beautiful of all the passages and first introduced to me by Camille and Gabriel when I went with them on a date. Was that weird? I mean, it didn't seem weird at the time but now I'm wondering if actually the whole thing was a strange omen for the love triangle we found ourselves in. But I was distracted by all the fun we were having and the beauty of my surroundings. Come here for the window displays.

– Passage Choiseul

A delightful covered arcade up by the Opéra, this quirky place, full of interesting shops and galleries, was where I decided to treat myself to a birthday stroll and enjoy all the lovely messages from home. There are restaurants, galleries, shops and even a theater. Lots of character and interesting details everywhere you look.

The passages are a very special feature of shopping in Paris. A completely charming relic of an older shopping world.

SHOPPING FASHION

I love to dress up to go shopping, and luckily Parisians do too. I met Sylvie shopping on the Rue Étienne Marcel, where there are lots of wonderful shops, and she looked completely fabulous as usual.

But as my American friend (and Friend of the Louvre) Judith Robertson said, it is also fine to go to the market in yoga pants, if that's what makes you feel comfortable.

I do like to wander about the designer shops and La Samaritaine in an elegant outfit, but if you are going on a big trip and intend to walk around a particular district or market, you should think about comfort.

- *Wear sneakers or flats with good cushioning for those cobbled streets.*

- *If you're going to be trying on a lot of clothes, wear something easy to take on and off. Jeans, sneakers, a crop top and a jacket is a reliable combination for shopping.*

- *Don't forget to take a large, light tote for packing away your goodies, and always take a few easy-to-stow string bags in case you see some delicious groceries that you simply have to buy!*

FRENCH BRANDS THAT 'PARISIENNES' ADORE

Big department stores are wonderful things, and you will have the benefit of lots of choice and dozens of labels under one roof. They are a one-stop shop, but of course the ranges on offer are limited because of space, and some brands don't put concessions (a small selection of their stock) into department stores. So you still have plenty of scope for going elsewhere to find your favorite fashion elements. Heroes on the main street that offer some amazing clothes at completely affordable prices include global brands like Zara, H&M and Mango, but there are also some French brands beloved of Parisian ladies. Search out these jewels…

Sézane

Lots of character, this boutique offers casual and boho style with a youthful elegance.

Balzac Paris

Chic and relaxed, with real Parisian style.

Sandro

Completely Parisian, this label is chic, elegant and refined, with muted colors and fluid lines, concentrating on cut and quality.

Isabel Marant

Famous for her taste and easy-to-wear classics with a twist, Isabel delivers fabulous and timeless French fashion.

Comptoir des Cotonniers

Celebrated for its pared-back elegance and very high quality, Parisians love this label's deceptively simple chic designs at affordable prices.

There are so many more! You can have a huge amount of fun finding your style and exploring the dozens and dozens of boutiques and shops hidden away throughout the city. And if you can't get to Paris, many of these brands have online stores.

SHOPPING DISTRICTS OF PARIS

LOUVRE AND TUILERIES

You'll find very expensive stores here, with many designers and high-end luxury boutiques catering to the most affluent of Parisians and visitors.

BOULEVARD HAUSSMANN & GRANDS BOULEVARDS

Here are the grand department stores in all their splendor, as well as plenty of other expensive shops. Visit this district in the holiday season to see the enchanting lights and window displays.

LE MARAIS

Shopping heaven. Here you'll find endless boutiques of all types, from high-end chic to quirky one-offs, thrift stores, art shops, galleries, artisan jewelry and cosmetics. There are famous names and new, exciting emerging labels. Hang out at cutting-edge store Merci, which has its own café and restaurant, as well as fashion, homewares and accessories, all displayed like a fabulous gallery.

AVENUE MONTAIGNE & CHAMPS-ÉLYSÉES

If you've been paying attention, you'll remember this is Paris's Golden Triangle, where you'll find the flagship shores of the ultimate luxury brands of Paris. The most wonderful window shopping in the world.

SAINT-GERMAIN-DES-PRÉS

Do what Sylvie does and explore the refined boutiques around this classy area. There are lots of bookshops and antique stores too, which is appropriate for an area that was the philosophical heart of Paris.

RUE DE RIVOLI

Find all the major chain stores in this area, along with the shopping area of Les Halles with its roster of familiar names. Less pure Paris, more global, there are a lot of brands around here that will be familiar to you, but you can still find some interesting one-off treasures.

FIND YOUR VINTAGE

I get huge pleasure from the creativity and variety of the mainstream clothes stores. I love their energy, their joy in fashion and their determination to provide up-to-the-minute catwalk trends at an affordable price. You can get such exciting looks and great quality too.

Then there is the happiness of finding those one-offs. Flea markets and vintage stores are my happy place, where I can easily lose myself for hours. There is nothing like the joy of finding hidden treasure – a designer piece in perfect condition or an amazing accessory that will add that special something to an outfit. The holy grail is finding a vintage piece that fits perfectly and is in mint condition, as well as being absolutely beautiful, and from a new and exciting designer – in other words, brand new and fashion-forward! *#youdontfindholygrailseveryday*

You will be able to discover amazing shops and boutiques all over Paris to satisfy your taste. It will not surprise you to learn that I'm drawn both to high-end and quirky, colorful and surprising, cute and sophisticated, zany and interesting, ideally all in one outfit. Paris is a dream come true and I spend so many hours swiping through rails and burrowing through heaps and exploring piles of items that are just begging to be given a new lease of life.

Here are some of my favorite Aladdin's caves, where there are all kinds of treasure to be discovered. *#opensesame #justcallmegenie*

VINTAGE CLOTHING PARIS, 11TH ARRONDISSEMENT
Exactly what it says – but better. This lovely little shop offers very classy designer dresses, embroidered coats, beaded bags and more, though of course you will have to look through the racks to find the treasure. But that is half the fun! Find your Chloé, Celine and YSL gems here!

CÉLIA DARLING VINTAGE, 9TH ARRONDISSEMENT
Was there ever a lovelier name for a vintage store? This boutique is just my cup of tea, exactly the place I'll find something amazing to finish off an outfit. The owner is a specialist with a trained artistic eye, so you will find treasure wherever you look. The clothes are from 1940s to 1990s and yet the looks are incredibly modern, which is exactly what I want!

PRISCA PARIS, MONTMARTRE
Luxe is everything here – you'll find pieces by the great designers of the last century plus gorgeous accessories. If you crave some Dior and YSL, this is your piece of heaven! But there's lots more on offer – Hermès and Chanel to name but two – so come and find some genuine *mode à la Paris*.

VINTAGE DÉSIR, LE MARAIS
This dusty and chaotic little shop might not offer the kind of luxe you get with designers, but you will find a huge selection of vintage clothes, with lots of jackets, coats and accessories that can provide a building block or a finishing touch for your expensive pieces, and you'll spend happy hours looking for them too.

MAMIE BLUE, 9TH ARRONDISSEMENT
This vintage store offers true old-world style. You'll only find dressy pieces here, gorgeous and high quality too. These are the kind of things you can rock for a big occasion, so come ready to shake your movie star tail feathers!

CHINEMACHINE, 9TH ARRONDISSEMENT

Come here for your kooky and eccentric pieces that will get everyone talking. Thigh-high boots and clothes made of unexpected items mean you'll find a talking-point piece that will astonish everyone. Just the thing for the added dash of interest that I 🏎.

ROSEMARKET VINTAGE, 9TH ARRONDISSEMENT

My favorite kind of vintage – haute couture with the kind of fashion names to make your mouth water. Think Chanel, Dior, Givenchy … You will find heaps of gorgeous labels and the most beautiful, timeless, chic clothes: suits, coats, dresses, jackets and purses, all in perfect condition. I've gone to heaven.

THANX GOD I'M A V.I.P., 10TH ARRONDISSEMENT

That is the actual name, I'm not just saying it! I'm not a VIP obviously, but I have hung out with a few. But honestly, you'll feel like a VIP as you go through the rails of amazing designer clothes. And here's the USP: it's all been color-coordinated for easy browsing. I'm dying here! It couldn't be easier to mix, match and clash your favorite shades AND your favorite labels. What's not to love? The owners have twenty years' experience of Parisian fashion and it shows in their totally cool, must-visit boutique.

FLEA MARKETS

Who doesn't love a flea market, or marché aux puces? They prove the old adage that one woman's trash is another woman's amazing vintage find that will provide the most wonderful finishing touch to her home.

In Paris, flea markets are practically little towns in themselves, and you will find yourself inspired by hours spent browsing among the vast spread of trinkets and objects, all manner of curios and, of course, clothes and accessories. They are found a little further out, but will be worth the trip. Go in the morning for the best bargains and watch out for your belongings – there are plenty of pickpockets at work in the busy market.

– Les Puces de Montreuil

This is a little less well known than the others, but you'll find some wonderful bargains here, among all the usual antiques, objects and junk. Look for the little square where the best dealers are.

– Marché aux Puces de Saint-Ouen

This famous market started as a ragtag collection of stalls and is now a huge and much-visited market with 3,000 traders. It's actually a collection of smaller markets, each one devoted to its own speciality. My favorite is the Marché Vernaison, which offers more fashion, but you'll find ceramics, furniture, jewelry, artwork, vintage cameras, toys, lighting ... the list goes on and on. If you have enough French (unlike me), you may even be able to haggle and get a real bargain.

– Marché aux Puces de la Porte de Vanves

This weekend market is worth a visit for its antique clothes and piles of quirky and fascinating objects. I like to flip through the rails and look for that extra special something. You can find lots of beautiful vintage linen here.

EMILY'S WORK PARIS

Chapter 4

My whole raison for coming to Paris was work. When the Gilbert Group acquired Savoir, and Madeline got unexpectedly pregnant and couldn't go, it was a passport to living my dreams in the French capital.

Savoir is based in the Place de Valois in an office above the Galerie Patrick Fourtin. It's in a very beautiful and luxurious area of Paris, a few blocks from the Louvre and close to the luxury shopping district. I couldn't have imagined anywhere more quintessentially Parisian to work. I wanted to sigh with happiness every morning at first, as I soaked up the incredible surroundings. I truly could not believe I was going to work in this amazing place.

I guess I got so carried away with the aesthetics that I didn't exactly concentrate on the problems that were bound to arise.

I knew, from Savoir's perspective, I had some disadvantages. I didn't speak French. Or, as I said to Julien on my first day, 'You lost me at *bonjour*.'

But I did have enthusiasm, a willingness to learn, and I was confident about my skills in social media strategy. And I was cheerful! Very cheerful and very positive. That had to balance out the not-speaking-French thing. Right?

I was in for a shock. No one at Savoir wanted me *at all*. My bosses seemed certain I had nothing to teach the French. Nada.

Perhaps the most difficult part of my journey in Paris has been my struggle to understand my workplace. The hostility I felt from the people I most wanted to please was horrible! At a time when I was far from home, had just broken up with Doug and had no friendly shoulders to cry on, Sylvie made it clear she hated me and every word that came out of my mouth. I had to protest sometimes, and remind her that we were on the same side!

As she memorably said: 'You come to Paris, you walk into my office, you don't even bother to learn the language ... perhaps we'll work together but no, we won't be friends.' I was so desperate for her to like me, I even considered taking up smoking for about five minutes. She did keep going on about having a cigarette and even gave me a cigarette case for my birthday. I mean, those things will kill you. No job is worth that.

Sylvie did learn to like me eventually (I think). But for a while she was adamant that I had nothing to offer.

It took some serious resolve not to break down completely. I carried on. I stayed true to what I believed in, while learning whatever I could from those who knew better. I improved my French (slowly, very slowly) and I started to figure out how this crazy world of French luxury operated and how my American ideas would best work in this arena.

I also gave up a few hopeless struggles.

And I learned a lot along the way, about so much more than just work. In the end, I began to think in a new way and it has been exciting to open my eyes to different attitudes, ideas and values. I even learned to break some rules occasionally. I know. Pretty out of character!

Luc's Wisdom

♥ Don't be early!

SAVOIR
PARIS

GALERIE PATRICK FOURTIN

Not speaking French was the disadvantage I was most worried about, but as it turned out, that wasn't the area of greatest confusion. Parisians, mostly, have a very good standard of English. It was really unusual to discover that Patricia, who was in charge of social media output, had no knowledge of the language at all. But that was lucky for me as it gave me a specific role. It was everything else that was a problem. Everything.

For one thing, the company is in an eighteenth-century house, not the kind of modern office building that I was used to. I didn't mind that, I loved the beautiful setting and the antique windows and the parquet floors, and so on. But I was pretty amazed to ascend to our floor in a tiny iron elevator with no actual proper walls or doors. It was like climbing into a little cage and then someone somewhere winching it up. Different. Very different.

Then there was the lack of air conditioning, and the general sense that being in lovely surroundings was way more important than having an efficient and comfortable workplace. It was my first clue that French priorities are very different to American ones.

My second was when I met the owner of Savoir, Mr Brossard. He was smoking and greeted me with kisses on both cheeks before telling me I had nothing to offer.

Not speaking French was the disadvantage I was most worried about.

Smiling or stupid?

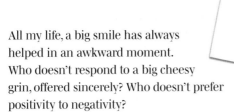

All my life, a big smile has always helped in an awkward moment. Who doesn't respond to a big cheesy grin, offered sincerely? Who doesn't prefer positivity to negativity?

I arrived at Savoir full of good cheer. And no one seemed to like it AT ALL. I got so confused at first. I was used to being an upbeat and well-liked colleague with a positive attitude. Now everyone looked like they wanted to slap me. They disagreed with everything I said and stood for.

They're very disagreeable, Mindy said, as a joke. But it wasn't much comfort.

Eventually Sylvie even said, 'Stop smiling so much, everyone will think you're stupid.'

And that helped because I realized I had to tone it down just a little to get taken seriously. Obviously, I still smile and I still believe in positivity at work (and in life!).

And I like to think that my smiling was also catching. Luc and Julien started smiling back at me (when Julien wasn't furious with me for taking over clients ... whoops). I've even caught Sylvie with the corners of her mouth lifting once or twice.

#wondersnevercease
#smileandtheworldsmileswithyou
#victoryforAmericathistime

TO WORK OR NOT TO WORK

When I arrived at Savoir, I was determined to show that I'm a conscientious employee. I love my career and I want to do my absolute best at all times. I kind of assumed that this would make me a valuable member of the team and that they would like me for working hard – that's how it always went back home. The more I worked, the better things went for me and the more Madeline valued me.

So it was a huge surprise to discover that my co-workers seemed to want to do all they could to stop me from working so much. In fact, it almost seemed to offend them.

I was really confused! Were jobs in France not the same as jobs in America? I quickly discovered that they are most certainly not. *#twotribes*

HOW TO FIT INTO SAVOIR

- Turn up late after fitting in some shopping.
- Look impossibly chic.
- Drink black coffee, and don't have any food at your desk.
- Go outside for a cigarette every hour.
- Head off for lunch at noon.
- Return from lunch at 3 p.m.
- Plan your social life and evening engagements.
- Leave at 6 p.m. for a glamorous work party.
- Go out for dinner afterwards and flirt with clients.
- Repeat.

SAVOIR
PARIS

WHAT'S THE TIME, MR WOLF?

My colleagues' timekeeping is completely at odds with what I was used to.

On my first full day, I arrived at 8.30 a.m., ready to start. No one else arrived until 10.30 a.m. When Julien found me pacing up and down outside, wondering what the hell was going on, he looked like I was the one with the problem for wanting to start working at a reasonable hour.

I guess the time difference means that the States doesn't wake up until after lunch, so my busy time in terms of international communications is often in the afternoon. And to be honest, no one really answers a phone or reads an email at Savoir before 10 a.m., so I'm beginning to see the point of not rushing in.

But how does anyone get all the work done?

Sylvie regularly arrives at 11 a.m. and goes out for a very long lunch not long after that. And yet, mysteriously, despite never seeming to try too hard, she is really good at her job and always on top of everything, so I suppose that when she is in the office, she is really there. Completely there. Doing what she needs to do. And when she walks out the door, she thinks about other things, I suppose, and lives her life.

Interesting idea.

Except... indulge me here... the French that I've worked with blur lines in their work life that we would never blur in America. I like to keep my professional life and personal life separate. It's different here. Sylvie carried on an affair with Antoine Lambert for years and never raised the rates that Savoir was charging Maison Lavaux, and that seemed to be fine. No one even noticed until Madeline arrived.

Nor did anyone seem to think it was inappropriate that Antoine gave me that La Perla underwear as a gift – they were mainly worried that it would upset Sylvie – or bat an eyelid when he sent Sylvie those nipple rings at work. Then, after she and Antoine were over, Sylvie had a fling with Erik the photographer and immediately hired him for a major campaign as though that wasn't a conflict of interest. No one cared!

How does anyone
get any work
done?

That puzzled me. My colleagues might insist on not taking the office home or to parties, but they sure do like to bring their personal life into the office. #baffled #Frenchparadox

Julien's Wisdom

♡ `Boring is worse than basic`

All the time, I was being told to lighten up, and felt like I was very uptight and just needed to relax a little. But here's the crazy thing: the French have tons and tons of rules!

For example, there are very firm rules about when and where they will talk about work. It got to the point where I thought I was going to be banned from talking in the office. I could not talk about work at parties even when they were parties expressly held for work.

When I started to talk about social media strategy to Antoine at the launch of De l'Heure, everyone looked astonished. Sylvie was more than astonished, she was outraged. She said, 'Oh *mon dieu*, you know we're at a soirée, not a conference call!' At Camille's château, I was rebuked by her mother Louise for talking about work at the dinner table, even though my visit was to help understand how Savoir could help their champagne-producing business. I can maybe see the case for that, but what's the harm in sharing all my ideas? And Louise didn't seem very keen on talking to me at other times either, unless it was about how Timothée stacked up as a lover. And that seemed pretty inappropriate to me.

And when I tried to get people to talk to me about work when I was in Saint-Tropez on the weekend, well … now, they said, it was actually *against the law*.

May I eat in the office? Absolutely not.
Can my private post remain private? Er … no, it can't.
There are rules, all right – just different ones.
Sometimes, just occasionally, the rules worked in my favor.

It was a horrible shock when Sylvie fired me. And then Luc and Julien thought it was nothing at all. Apparently, it's impossible to fire someone in France because of the bureaucracy. The paperwork takes YEARS according to Julien, and they said just keep coming in and don't believe her.

But they were right – I just pretended I hadn't been fired and eventually it turned out okay for me. In America, my desk would have been cleared in five minutes, the paperwork done in thirty, and my severance paid the same day. Within a week, they'd have replaced me and forgotten me altogether. So I guess there are upsides.

But if you don't have the right paperwork, nothing can happen. Mindy didn't have the right visa and that condemned her to a life as Dame Pipi. Even if she was the most glamorous and talented toilet attendant ever, slaying her numbers at the club. And it meant that her next career move was busking – until she, Benoît and Étienne were able to get a gig at the Shangri-La. She will still have to work out that paperwork one day, though, or it could mean she has to return to China after all …

When I asked her if we needed a permit to hold my birthday party outside our apartment in the little square opposite, she said, 'If we ask, we will!' So we didn't ask. And that seemed to sum it up pretty well.

BALANCE TON PORC

It has to be said that I have felt at times that a line can get crossed at work in Paris.

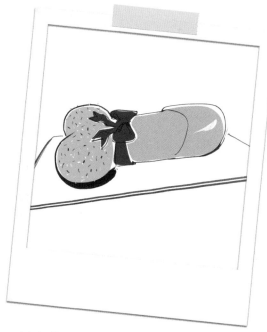

The French take on *#MeToo* is *#BalanceTonPorc* – literally, get rid of your pig – or denounce your oppressor. It has started the kind of cultural change here that we've seen in workplaces all over the world, where women are finally realizing that they don't have to put up with harassment, and that there's safety in numbers and in bringing things out into the open.

My colleagues and clients are maybe not quite as quick to see that things they consider acceptable are not going to fly with an international audience. But that is why Savoir needed me – to translate for them what wasn't going to chime with an American market. A woman in the nude walking for the enjoyment of clothed men isn't going to look like empowerment to us, it's going to look like exploitation. *#sexyorsexist* was one of my biggest contributions to the conversation, and I hope it helps the whole debate over what is acceptable, even though at first they called me the prude police.

Luc and Julien are adorable but they don't seem to have heard of workplace harassment. Luc is fine with returning the Gilbert Group corporate commandments that Madeline sent me with a huge picture of a penis firmly drawn right over the top. The two of them are happy demonstrating sex positions. Is it appropriate? They don't seem to mind!

I guess that since I got my own back with a penis-shaped cake, I'm no angel. But it made them laugh and respect me just a little. So it was worth it. *#ifyoucantbeatem* But I'm sure things will change here – for the better.

Mindy's Wisdom

The wonderful thing about Paris is that no one judges you for doing nothing. It's practically an art form here

NO CAN DO

It's true that there is a weird *pas possible* attitude here that makes no sense to me.

Why would a florist not sell you their expensive roses?

Why does a plumber expect coffee and a croissant before he will do you the courtesy of explaining he can't fix your shower for maybe weeks, and really doesn't care about that? (I guess the upside was that I had to share Gabriel's *douche*. Shower, that is.) ☺

Why does your concierge tell you she is *trop occupée* – too busy – to help you with any of the things you thought it was her job to do?

Just like with shopkeepers and businesses closing for the busy month of August (see my rant about this in Chapter 6), it just doesn't make any sense to me. It doesn't gel with my American attitude toward work at all. We like to devote our lives to our jobs and taking time off is something we feel guilty for. But the French have lots of vacations, take long lunch hours, and some of them are firmly of the opinion that not only do they deserve this, but also that working is actually something of a chore.

And only in Paris will you be sacked from a job because of the wrong charm hanging from your handbag. And you have to persuade some people that Instagram is not a term of abuse!

Here I've found that how people feel about things is sometimes more important than money.

I guess it is a creative industry, and it sure is full of artistic temperaments. It's my job, very often, to negotiate that and say oui! And *c'est possible* – it's possible – instead of *non*.

MY SECRETS FOR SUCCESS

- If you want to win new business, don't be afraid to grab your target – I wouldn't let Randy Zimmer, the hotel chain owner, walk away; I knew he had to listen.

- Get their attention fast, ideally with charm. Smiles are good!

- Don't take no for an answer, unless you really have to.

- Do your research – it always impresses people and shows you really care. Olivia Thompson, the CMO of Durée, told me my passion was obvious, and that I cared more for the brand than just for swag bags. *#winning*

- Have your ideas ready to deliver and make them short, sharp and snappy! It's called an elevator pitch – something you can say in the time it takes an elevator to get from the ground floor to the top of the building where the head honchos work. I used this in the short time I had to get Randy Zimmer to listen to me and it worked.

- Have your business card at hand so they take your details away in their pocket or purse.

- Accept when you've reached the end – I knew Olivia Thompson was not coming back to Savoir and it was time to bow out gracefully.

- Know your products back to front.

- Harness the power of social media – it's a language we can all speak!

- Keep on top of your social media: fresh content keeps attention.

- Curate your content – make sure you have quantity *and* quality.

- Tag as much as possible for maximum reach.

- Be positive and tell an interesting story.

- Avoid clichés and lazy ideas.

- You can get a bit crazy with social media (like the influencer who does the splits for her followers, or another whose dog runs the account) or you can stay quirky and humorous – I try to do the latter!

- Use your intelligence to stand out from the crowd; don't be afraid to be clever.

- Dream your best dreams!

- Don't overpromise and under-deliver (copyright: Sylvie).

Luc's Wisdom

Americans have the wrong balance. You live to work, we work to live.

I enjoy work and results. Gabriel has the kind of work ethic I understand. Chefs work so hard. When I met Camille's friends at the hammam spa, they told me I should never date a French chef because they are too devoted to their jobs, but that is a mindset I feel totally comfortable with. Where other people said *pas possible*, Gabriel said *oui*, even when I asked him to bake me eighty little cakes for the next day so that we could put on that show at Versailles. He was can-do, even though it would mean working through the night.

One of Camille's complaints to Gabriel was that he worked too hard and that he refused to mix his business with his personal life, but I totally got that. I would never tell Gabriel he works too hard. I applaud him for it, and when we worked together, we got amazing results. *#greatteam*

SYNTHESIS

If you're in my line of work, here are some hints!

- **Always think creatively and out of the box** – my idea for a champagne you *don't* drink was one of my favorite moments.

- **Match ideas and clients and see what kind of exciting collabs you can create:**

  1. *Perfumier with hotelier = signature scent for a chain of luxury hotels!*
  2. *Suitcases with a designer = brand refresh!*
  3. *Take your clients to a new young chef's restaurant = new brand to promote when they invest in it!*
  4. *Get two feuding fashion friends back together = fantastic publicity and brand symbiosis!*

- **And remember:** building a luxury brand takes time; don't worry if things don't work right away.

WORK COMMANDMENTS

I have to be honest: I like rules. I like them so much, I proposed a toast to them at Camille's château. The others seemed a bit bemused but they joined in. I like things tidy and I like life to be neat. Expectations should be explicit so that we all know where we stand.

I also know what it's like to be outside looking in, and I think that means that knowing how to fit in is important.

When I passed the Gilbert Group corporate commandments around, it went down very badly. These were the ones in particular that they seemed to hate:

1. *Thou shalt always maintain a positive attitude*
2. *Thou shalt always be on time*
3. *Thou shalt always praise in public and criticize in private*
4. *Avoid workplace romances*

'You told French people this? No wonder they hate you!' Mindy said. But I really couldn't see what was wrong with all of this. Maybe it was the tone?

But then, once Madeline arrived from Chicago, I began to see things in a different light. She worked according to the rules I was familiar with, but after spending months immersed in the French work culture, I was beginning to see things a little differently.

Madeline, who had been my hero and inspiration at home, suddenly seemed a bit … unsophisticated.

Her American habit of eating and drinking at her desk and on the move – and all the time, really, given that she was pregnant – began to seem really out of place. I suddenly understood why Sylvie had said with exasperation that I was always eating. And why she banned food in the office (unless she had just had really great sex the night before, in which case we were allowed croissants). Food at the desk looks messy and out of place. Kind of gauche.

I can't believe I said that about lovely Madeline. Obviously I still adore her. But her approach seemed impersonal and sometimes even … rude?

Let them eat croissants!

But her values just didn't chime with French ones. She was more concerned with profit than success. And when the entire office walked out and left just the two of us to cope, her attitude really surprised me. She didn't mind that priceless experience had just resigned, maybe destroying the entire company in the process, along with all the hard work we had put into nurturing brand relationships and growing their businesses.

She wanted young, cheap workers she could mold into copies of herself as soon as possible. Not the kind of people who go to cemeteries on their lunch break, or who dress flamboyantly and adore fashion, or who flounce around and take the office out for two-hour lunches with wine, or who cry with joy when they land a great client, or … I could go on.

I thought Savoir was dysfunctional until I saw it without all the amazing people who make it what it is. Then it really was dysfunctional because it just couldn't function. In fact, it didn't exist at all. *#cestvrai #itstrue*

Antoine's Wisdom

Now that you're in Paris, you'll find that the most wonderful things exist outside your box

I'm super excited that Sylvie is going to set out on her own and become the kick-ass boss and company owner that I know she can be. And believe me, I was beyond flattered when she offered me a job. Who would have guessed that after all that, all the times she wanted me OUT and GONE and accused me of being the problem … When she told me I only spoke the obvious … or couldn't help screwing up ….

Well.

It was just the biggest compliment of my life when someone with as high standards as Sylvie thought I was worth something, and not because I was her mini-me, the kind that Madeline wanted rooms full of. But because I WAS me. With all my flaws and all my good points.

So what am I going to choose?
#watchthisspace
#dotdotdot

Julien's Wisdom

Happy endings are very American

HOW TO COPE WITH A BOSS LIKE SYLVIE

- Don't say 'Hey girl!' when you see her – she hates it.

- Don't take her expensive roses.

- Be very suspicious when she tells you not to come in until 11 a.m. – she might be planning to swipe an important client away from you.

- Carry her shopping if she wants you to.

- Be discreet about her affairs and sympathetic when she's suffering.

- Always say you're on it!

- Apologize – but not too much.

- Sometimes don't talk, just listen.

- Don't give in! She'll like you eventually … I think!

Useful work vocabulary

No, please, let me make the coffee.
Non, s'il vous plaît, c'est moi qui fais le café.

I'll get on that right away.
Oui, je fais ça tout de suite.

May I please attend this meeting?
Puis-je assister à la réunion?

Have you stolen my client?
Tu as piqué mon client?

Is that gift entirely appropriate?
Est-ce que ce cadeau est approprié?

That gift is wildly inappropriate!
Ce cadeau est complètement inapproprié!

I have a confession . . .
Je dois vous avouer quelque chose . . .

Don't worry, I'll fix it!
Ne vous inquiétez pas, je m'en occupe!

It is vacation time again?
C'est déjà les vacances?

Where is everyone?
Où est passé tout le monde?

EMILY'S SECRET PARIS

Chapter 5

Paris is the most exciting city in the world; you never know what's going to happen next

Paris is both an open book and a vast collection of amazing secrets. You will already be familiar with its most iconic sites and symbols. There's the Eiffel Tower, as ever. There is no sight like it, standing four-footed over Paris, the ultimate expression of this awesome city and its sophistication. It makes me smile whenever I see it. In the morning, it is stern and black, silhouetted against the soft Parisian sky as the sun rises over the Sacré Coeur in the east. In the evenings it sparkles against the navy blue of the night as the sun sinks down over the Bois de Boulogne in the west. Then it lights up and twinkles on the hour every hour for five minutes, as though it has slipped on a sequinned jacket, a sight that still gives me the shivers. (Also, you might want to know that it sparkles one last time at 1 a.m., and for a full ten minutes – the perfect backdrop to making out).

You'll also probably have seen the Louvre with its amazing glass pyramid; the tricolore fluttering above the Palais de Justice; Notre-Dame; the Arc de Triomphe … All the go-to symbols of Paris. When you visit Paris, you must see these places, that goes without saying. But there are so many not-so-well-known places to enjoy that will bring the character of this awesome city alive and give you a very special insight into what makes it so magical.

You will also have so much fun creating your own adventures and looking behind the scenes into secret Paris.

'You're clearly under the influence of this city. You're high on Paris!'
– OLIVIA THOMPSON, CMO OF DURÉE

#HighonParis

SECRET PLACES
TO EAT

LA MAISON ROSE

Pretty. Pink. Delicious food. What more could you want? Mindy brought me to this lovely little hidden gem when I needed a friend to talk to about Sylvie and my troubles at work, and the whole place cheered me up like nothing else. The charming exterior is sugar pink, with contrasting mint-green shutters and bistro furniture. The menu is eco-conscious, with a farm-to-table concept. Have a slice of chocolate *tarte* scattered with soft white sugar and a spoonful of tangy *crème fraîche*.

HÔTEL PARTICULIER

This beautiful Montmartre restaurant is where I met with Olivia Thompson to discuss becoming an influencer. I had to turn down her kind offer, of course, as my loyalty was to Savoir. I was disappointed when I didn't manage to convince her to come back as a client, but you can't win them all. I fell in love with this irresistibly Instagrammable restaurant, and I hear the brunch is incredible.

LULU LA NANTAISE

I came to this hidden gem with Thomas, Camille and Gabriel during our double date. We sat outside so that the men could smoke, although it was Gabriel who was smoldering with irritation when Thomas casually said he expected a chef to roll his own cigarettes and looked rather scornful when Gabriel said he did not. That did not exactly enhance the evening, but I still loved this pretty place right by the Canal Saint-Martin.

TORTUGA

This is where Camille asked me to meet her to make up after her – shall we say – frosty response to finding out about me and Gabriel. It's a chic restaurant on the rooftop of the Galeries Lafayette, and it is known for its fish dishes, but I wasn't really able to concentrate on the food, or on the amazing view of the Palais Garnier just behind me. But if you are not in the process of making promises you're not sure you can keep, then you might be able to enjoy it more than I was able to.

RALPH'S

The best cure for homesickness I found was Ralph Lauren's restaurant, where Judith from the American Friends of the Louvre took me. I don't know what was better, the menu being in English, or the cheeseburger that almost reduced me to tears. Strongly recommended to any American in Paris, particularly if *a certain someone* has disposed of your frozen deep-dish pizza sent to you all the way from Chicago.

What more
could you
want?

DEEP PAN PIZZA Co

La Maison Rose

SECRET PLACES TO HAVE FUN

Much as we all want to see the famous sights, it's not always pleasant to feel part of a crowd. If you want to know what I mean, try going to the Louvre to see the Mona Lisa at midday at the height of tourist season. You won't be able to get near.

Sometimes it makes sense to take a different approach. My handy hint for the Louvre is to go in the evenings – on Wednesdays and Fridays it's open till 9.45 p.m. – or near closing time on a regular day. Last entry is often up to an hour before the museum actually shuts, but most people will be on their way out by then. If you know what you want to see, you can go straight to it and the crowds will be gone. *#thankmelater* (Be warned: no Insta stories here! You can't take any photos on your mobile phone while there, sadly. *#missedopportunity*)

Alternatively, try one of the many smaller art museums around Paris that have wonderful works of art but are nowhere near as crowded. You will still see some Picassos, Delacroix, Monets and the rest, but in less hectic surroundings.

Here are some other fun ideas:

- For a special hideaway afternoon, go to the Bois de Vincennes, take a boat on the Lac Daumesnil and land at the island in the middle. You can eat at the Châlet des Îles, a real Swiss chalet put on the island in the nineteenth century. No one will find you there!

- Le Musée de la Vie Romantique is an utterly delightful museum in Montmatre dedicated to the romantic life of George Sand, and in the pretty garden is the Rose Bakery, which serves teatime treats. So quaint and hidden away. But maybe I like it because of the color scheme: palest pink with green shutters and ornate ironwork.

- Musée des Arts Forains is a fun-fair museum full of vintage carousels and other antique fairground rides. This is where we held the amazing party to promote the launch of Fourtier watches. Everyone had a great time trying out the rides, and looked amazing in their party outfits! I wish I could have enjoyed it a little more, but my anxiety about the Fourtier watch kind of took the shine off. I definitely want to go back, though, and recommend that you visit too.

- Buy something to read at Shakespeare & Company, the famous English-language bookshop on the Left Bank opposite Notre-Dame, then wander to the Jardin du Luxembourg, find a shady bench and enjoy your new book. Maybe get a takeout coffee and a piece of *gâteau* as a treat as well...

GARDEN RESTAURANTS IN PARIS

Garden restaurants have a wonderful, secret feeling, and are soothing oases in the middle of the busy city. You'll find cute places to visit in all the parks and gardens of Paris.

Here are just a few:

- Visit the **Café des Marronniers** (the café of the chestnut trees) in the Tuileries Garden and sip a *chocolat chaud* in the shade of the chestnut trees, with all the sights of Paris in front of you.

- For an added dose of culture, try the garden restaurant in the grounds of the **Musée Rodin**, where Rodin's sculptures sit poetically nearby as you dine.

- Go to **Les Belles Plantes** in the Jardin des Plantes, Paris's botanical garden. You can eat ceviche and a light salad here while surrounded by plants and flowers – not just real ones, but also in the wallpaper and décor. The ultimate garden restaurant, and a great secret too.

Le Jardin des Plantes

Musée Rodin

Instant fun!

- When it gets dark, visit the tourist stalls in the **Latin Quarter** and buy silly hats and street food, before getting a drink at **La Grille Montorgueil** as the night draws on.

- Ride the carousel under the **Eiffel Tower**.

- Give your best friend a piggyback around the black-and-white-striped columns known as the **Colonnes de Buren**, an art installation in front of the Palais-Royal. Call Mindy if you need someone to help you out!

- Eat ice cream in front of the **Place de l'Odéon**.

- Find a crêpe stall and choose your favorite filling to eat on the steps in front of the **Sacré Coeur**. Take some champagne to make it extra special and watch the sun come up over Montmartre.

- Find the street performers, mime artists and buskers who are performing all over Paris and enjoy a wonderful show. Just remember to put a few euros in the hat to say merci! You might find Mindy, Étienne and Benoît doing their thing if you're lucky!

- Find the **Paris Plages**, or beach, a sandy stretch set up by the Seine from July to September. Put on your bikini, order a cool drink, play pétanque on the sand, and plunge into a pool. If you ignore the noise of the traffic, you could almost be at the seaside, right?

- Go see the dinosaurs at the **Natural History Museum** in the **Jardin des Plantes**. Everyone feels better when they've seen a mammoth skeleton.

SEXY, SECRET PARIS

Sex is no secret in Paris, everyone knows that! You can get a rush of sexy romance by going to look at the famous sculpture *The Kiss* by Auguste Rodin at the Musée Rodin, a gorgeous little museum but not exactly a secret. Lots of people want to see that statue, which is not surprising.

But there are some interesting after-hours places to go which aren't so well known, so if you are in the mood for some naughty fun, here's an idea or two for you...

♡ Le Crazy Horse

Presenting a show with athletic, graceful, beautiful, barely dressed female dancers, this club has been around for seventy years and played a huge role in developing the burlesque and cabaret scene. It celebrates playful and clever sauciness with a heady mix of music, dance, costume and lights – and it's very sexy!

♡ Le Raidd

A gay club where the male body is worshiped. You'll find stunning men showing their incredible physiques, flexing impressive muscles and picking up tips from customers like Grégory Duprée, who likes nothing more than an evening paying homage to all the beauty on display.

♡ La Nouvelle Eve

A buzzing drag club where Mindy got her first break, even though she had to be the toilet attendant. But no one was expecting Dame Pipi to stand up and deliver 'Dynamite' the way she did! The drag queens are amazing and you'll have a ball here.

♡ Roxie

A supper club with live music. If you're after a sophisticated, high-end sexy establishment, you'll listen to smoky singing in the dark and seductive red and black surroundings, and late in the night you'll be dancing to the irresistible jazz and R&B.

It celebrates
playful and
clever sauciness –
and it's very sexy!

Le Crazy Horse

SECRET
GRANDEUR

It's not hard to find secret grandeur in Paris. It's everywhere you look, in fact – you just might not know what you are seeing. If you walk through the streets of Saint-Germain-des-Prés, where Sylvie lives, as previously mentioned, you will pass door after glossy door, each one firmly closed. Behind them lie exquisite courtyards and lavish apartments where some truly sumptuous lifestyles are to be found. But they are all secret.

You can get a little closer to the secret grandeur of Paris if you are lucky. My job takes me into the heart of the most glamorous locations in Paris, and I know how fortunate I am to see these amazing places close up. I will never forget having a front-row seat at the show in Versailles in the stunning Hall of Mirrors. Those Marie Antoinette-style models, all shapes and sizes, their skirt cages decorated in flowers, pastel wigs on their heads, and amazing Duprée shapewear making them sleek and smooth. When they broke into a dance, it was something else.

But most unforgettable of all was the entrance of Pierre Cadault, dressed like a turquoise Sun King, taking his place on a throne at the show and ending the feud with his protégé. It was unforgettable.

You see what I mean? I know I'm fortunate to get such a thrilling behind-the-scenes peek, but come with me and you will too…

HÔTEL D'ÉVREUX

This stunning private mansion is on one of the most exclusive squares in Paris, the Place Vendôme in the 1st arrondissement. The square is also home to the Ritz Paris, which I've already told you about, and is instantly recognizable for its imposing verdigris column, which was erected by Napoleon to celebrate his victory at Austerlitz. 'Hôtel' in French does not always mean hotel the way we mean it – if it is a *hôtel particulier*, then it means a large and imposing private townhouse. The Place Vendôme is surrounded by hotels, but only one or two are actually hotels as we would understand them. I know, I know … typically French and confusing …

The Hôtel d'Évreux is for hire, which is how Durée Cosmetics came to be using it for the launch of its collection, to which I was invited as an influencer. A junior one, but still an influencer. I'll never forget seeing Olivia Thompson standing against that window with the Vendôme Column behind her. I had a real 'am I really in Paris?' moment, as I got the sensation of being allowed in somewhere that not many people are permitted to see.

CAFÉ DE L'HOMME

This beautiful space is where Antoine Lambert and Maison Lavaux launched De l'Heure, their sexy new fragrance. I had just arrived in Paris and was still finding my feet. As a result, I was blown away by the glamorous surroundings and the incredible Trocadéro, which gave me the most stunning view of the Tower getting its twinkle on.

I think maybe Antoine mistook my breathless wonder for complete naïveté and thought I would be an easy target. Perhaps he hoped to add me to his collection of Savoir conquests. What did he say to me again? Oh yes: 'You need to find yourself a nice French boyfriend. That's the best way to learn the language ... in bed.' But I wasn't going to give in that easily. And anyway, I came to Paris to work, not be seduced. Or fall in love. Or any of that. And you can see how successful I was at sticking to that resolution. *#hahaha*

HÔTEL PLAZA ATHÉNÉE

I don't think that in ordinary life I would ever have found myself sitting down in the Haute Couture Suite in one of the grandest fashion hotels in Paris. Fourtier had reserved it for Brooklyn Clark, the movie star, so that she could be a brand ambassador for their watches. I guess movie stars must get this kind of treatment all the time because she seemed completely blasé about getting her own massive suite in the heart of Paris and didn't even give the grand piano a second look! I mean, okay, maybe she can't play the piano, but couldn't she at least have tried 'Chopsticks' or something?

She was just as casual about having a whole rack of Pierre Cadault clothes to choose from. It was a little embarrassing, if I'm honest, when she kept dismissing these magnificent designer creations with barely concealed scorn. I suppose you get kind of spoiled if you're a star. Much later, I was privileged enough to see the suite in a totally different state: overflowing ashtrays, discarded bottles, clothing thrown about the room and lamps overturned. It wasn't quite rock-star-level destruction, but it was a mess. It showed that Brooklyn enjoyed herself though, and I got to see Suite 361 in a way I doubt I will again. Thank goodness ...

ATELIER PIERRE CADAULT

Talking of behind the scenes, how many people actually get to go inside the extraordinary workshop of creativity and excellence that is the *atelier* of a famous designer? Very few designers are allowed to call their work haute couture, but Pierre is one, and the honor of going to his creative space was a little overwhelming. I think that was why I didn't exactly cover myself with glory when we first met. I was nervous. But Pierre was at his worst. He has an artistic temperament and is prone to being a little condescending when he is ill at ease. As a result, I didn't warm to him even while Sylvie and Julien were prostrating before his genius. Which led to the infamous insult of *ringarde* being thrown my way. Of course I was mortified, but

that wasn't the real Pierre. When he isn't throwing epic temper tantrums, and everything that's on his desk as well, he's really very sweet and has a great sense of humor. I feel very privileged that these days I'm welcome in that large, light and beautiful space where Pierre puts his genius to work.

A BOX AT THE OPÉRA

It's thanks to Pierre that I got to see one of the VIP boxes at the Palais Garnier. He had designed the costumes for *Swan Lake* and it was my onerous duty to dress up to the nines and try to ambush Pierre so that he would forgive me for the crime of having that Eiffel Tower charm on my purse. I wasn't quite sure what I was going to do, but with the help of lucky timing, I was able to walk right into one of the lavish red velvet boxes and talk to Pierre before he sat down for the ballet. If I hadn't happened to mention *Gossip Girl*, the outcome could have been different, but it turned out that he was as big a fan of the series as I was. Maybe more! And I think my passionate speech about how ordinary girls crave a piece of the extraordinary, no matter how small, touched his heart. It reminded him that he needs girls like me to be his fans. We are the bedrock.

The box was extraordinary, hung with red velvet tassels and glittering with gold. From there I could see the ceiling, which was painted by Marc Chagall. You might not be able to get into a VIP box at the Opéra – and I wasn't there for long myself – but if you do get to Paris, you can take a tour of the opera house for a taste of all its amazing opulence.

SECRET
SOLACE

Even in Paris, life isn't all about fun and games and glamour and sex. There are times when things are bleak, your heart is sore, and you need to find some solace and retreat from the world for a while. Luckily, I have Luc as a friend, someone who might be obsessed with sex but who also has an outlook of French realism – romantic but shot through with pessimism. He has shown me a few ways to find some solace in Paris when I need some perspective.

Here some places you can go when you need a little peace and comfort:

LE PÈRE LACHAISE

This is the largest cemetery in Paris and the most visited in the world. Named after the confessor to King Louis XIV, it was the first-ever garden cemetery and is like a small town, with paved streets and many mausoleums that look like little houses. Maybe it comforts people to think that death is a bit like moving house: you will just have some new neighbors and less need for heating.

Le Père Lachaise is renowned for its notable occupants. Here you can find the graves of Chopin, Oscar Wilde, Édith Piaf, Jim Morrison and Gertrude Stein, among many others. And of course there is Balzac, author of *La Cousine Bette*. Which I haven't read yet, but I will. If you find Balzac's grave, I think you have a good chance of finding Luc there as well, munching on a baguette and contemplating death, something which seems to cheer him up. Lunch in a graveyard was also his idea of a birthday treat. #toeachhisown

> *There are times when things are bleak, your heart is sore, and you need to find some solace and retreat from the world for a while.*

OTHER PARISIAN CEMETERIES TO VISIT

– Montmartre Cemetery

After Napoleon decreed that no cemeteries could lie in the center of Paris, the old were emptied and new ones were created. This cemetery has many artists and performers because of its proximity to the artists' district of Montmartre. Visit if you'd like to see the graves of singers, musicians, dancers and artists, including Edgar Degas, Alexandre Dumas and Marie Duplessis, the inspiration for Dumas's 'La Dame aux Camélias', played by Greta Garbo in the famous movie 'Camille'.

– Montparnasse Cemetery

The southern cemetery is the second largest in Paris, and has politicians and philosophers among its inhabitants. Jean-Paul Sartre and Simone de Beauvoir are buried together here, under a headstone covered in lipstick kisses.

– Passy Cemetery

The most central of the Parisian cemeteries, you'll find Givenchy and Guerlain here, as well as Édouard Manet and other famous French names. The American socialite Natalie Barney is also here, a well-known twentieth-century lesbian who had an affair with the author Colette. Her life inspired the famous lesbian novel 'The Well of Loneliness'.

CINÉMA LE CHAMPO

Luc took me to this classic Parisian cinema to give me another view on French life and experience. Paris is 'the cinema capital of the world', as Luc says, and the first-ever public screening of a film took place here in 1895. But you are not going to see the kind of multiplexes you might be familiar with. True to form, Parisians prefer small, exclusive and chic, even with something glitzy like the movies, and style is everything.

Luc ate popcorn with me, which was a surprise because Parisians tend not to eat or drink while they watch movies. They adore art-house and vintage cinema and you will see lots of rereleases of classic movies all over the city, especially from the glory days of the *Nouvelle Vague* (New Wave), when French directors led the way in the art form and inspired a whole new way of telling stories through film.

Cinéma Le Champo is a Paris institution with a striking art-deco façade. Famed French film director Francois Truffaut himself came here. It was his masterpiece *Jules et Jim* that Luc brought me to see, a movie about a love triangle. I think he wanted to cheer me up, but I've got to admit, I did not feel more cheerful at the end. But I don't want to say why. *#nospoilershere*

But there is nothing like a trip to the movies to help take your mind off your troubles, and perhaps provide a bit of escapism and joy. *#notJuletsetJimthough*

OTHER PARISIAN CINEMAS TO VISIT

– La Pagode
A Paris secret on the Left Bank. This Japanese building was converted into a theater in the thirties and became a part of the cinema scene in the sixties, showing movies by Ingmar Bergman and Jean Cocteau. It is now an art-house cinema showing international films.

– Le Cinéma du Panthéon
Just around the corner from my apartment in the Latin Quarter is the oldest cinema in Paris. Once showcasing the 'Nouvelle Vague', it boats a cozy viewing salon designed by icon Catherine Deneuve. Not many cinemas can boast that kind of star power!

– Le Grand Rex
This marvelous cinema is not exactly a secret but it is still worth a visit. In fact, it can seat 2,800 people in its incredible art-deco viewing room. This is one of the places in Paris where you'll be able to see a blockbuster movie or two, and it hosts the big premieres as well. You'll find it in the middle of the city near the Grands Boulevards.

I want to see life, the
hero tortured for his love,
and the actress naked

Films with a Paris Vibe

Amélie

The Apartment

Gigi

Colette

Camille

The Three Musketeers

The Hunchback of Notre Dame

Les Misérables

An American in Paris

La Vie en Rose

Ratatouille

Moulin Rouge

Charade

Phantom of the Opera

Classic French Films

Jules et Jim

Les Parapluies de Cherbourg

Belle de Jour

À Bout de Souffle

Les Enfants du Paradis

Les Vacances de M. Hulot

Mon Oncle

Hiroshima Mon Amour

Jean de Florette

Manon des Sources

LE HAMMAM DE LA MOSQUÉE DE PARIS

When art and culture and food and beauty don't cut it anymore, it's time to relax, properly and thoroughly. Camille took me here to enjoy a sauna with her and her friends. What an amazing place! This oasis is dedicated to well-being and the art of living.

A hammam is a Turkish bath, open to the public. In the ancient world, before there was running water, these places provided a way to wash; there are ancient ruins of baths like this all over the world. At Pompeii two almost unscathed bathhouses were excavated, complete with the places for the customers to leave their shoes while they bathed or enjoyed hot steam rooms or cold plunge pools.

This beautiful hammam pays homage to the beauty and sensuality of the east. The steam room was deliciously warm and I was entranced by the gorgeous surroundings and the marvelous aromas. I just wish I could have relaxed a little more but, as you know, I'm not fully on board with the concept of letting it all out in the same way as Camille and her friends. I'm sure that's because I'm an uptight American, but hey, what can I do about it? I'm learning to be more French, but I may need a little more time before I'm *that* French.

ÉMILE ANTHOINE STADIUM

I grew up watching ball games, so I'm totally used to sitting in the bleachers and cheering on the guys as they fight for victory. I am, though, completely baffled by soccer. It looks simple enough – get the ball in the net while the other side tries to stop your team and get the ball in *their* net – but it is much more complicated than that apparently. Alfie was continually going on about something called 'offside'. Gabriel seemed to understand, but then a love of soccer – which they call football – is something that bonds the French and the British together.

There are bars all over town that show the big games and they are full to bursting with excitable guys shouting at the screen as they watch the teams kick their little white ball up and down a field. I'm still a baseball girl, which is why I got my local bar in Chicago to do a test commercial for my Champère idea. I wanted to know what they were cheering about. I know – I'm funny that way. *#gottabeincontrol*

But it's relaxing to watch sports, and we should have something like that to enjoy. It's a bright spot in our busy lives and bit of healthy running about is good for us. Of course, it's easy for me to say that from the stands, but I do go running, don't forget that!

PLAYGROUNDS

We're all big kids at heart, and it doesn't hurt to remember that from time to time. So go to the Jardin du Luxembourg and try out the Garnier merry-go-round (or carousel) designed by the architect who built the opera house – as you'd expect, it's a work of art. Then sail a toy boat in the Grand Bassin and eat an ice cream. Or for an eco-friendly ride, you can try the 1913 carousel in the Champs de Mars and ride one of the original wooden horses.

If it's a view you're after, the carousel in front of the Sacré Coeur gives you the most amazing vista of the city while you ride – I recommend it!

In the summer there is the Fête de Tuileries, when a fantastic fair runs for two months, with dozens of exciting rides, Ferris wheels, bumper cars, shooting galleries and halls of mirrors. Indulge your inner child with cotton candy, toffee apples, candied nuts, crêpes and donuts. OMG, I want all those things RIGHT NOW. *#sugarrush*

When autumn comes, the Fête du Bois de Boulogne starts, with over a hundred attractions, a Ferris wheel and bouncy castles, along with more adventurous rides. Get a grilled sandwich or some hot frites from one of the stalls and enjoy all the fun of the fair. *#bigkids #innocentfun*

All of this has made me think about the amazing richness of this wonderful city, where old and new, open and secret, exist side by side. It's a city that unashamedly exhorts you to enjoy yourself and to celebrate, to nourish yourself, body, soul and mind.

I've said it before, but really – there is nowhere like Paris.

Don't forget to let me know what secrets you discover!

EMILY'S ESCAPADES OUTSIDE PARIS

Chapter 6

As much as Parisians adore Paris, they do leave the city occasionally.

The thing that is strangest for Americans to understand is that they all seem to do it at the same time. In August, everyone goes *en vacances* (on vacation) and the city can appear to shut down, with dozens of shops and restaurants closed till September. That's the time when lots of tourists arrive to see this great city and it's typical of the way the French think that they decide they'd rather close their businesses at this busy time and go away in order to enjoy their summer, rather than capitalize on all those visitors.

But don't worry, there are still lots of places to go to if you do come to Paris in the summer. All the major sights are still open, plenty of cafés and restaurants are trading, and the city feels far from empty.

Paris in the summer has its own beauty. Its cool fountains and shady parks come into their own at that time of year. There is no better time for wandering into the Bois de Boulogne and finding somewhere for a delightful picnic under the trees, or a café with umbrellas to shade its tables, and while away a summer's day.

In fact, it was in the Jardin du Palais-Royal, a beautiful little park with a fountain near the Louvre, that I first met Mindy. We started talking on a bench under the lime trees.

I have to warn you though – air conditioning is a rarity here. In fact, the French positively discourage it. When, on a particularly hot day in the office, I asked about the AC, I couldn't believe it when Julien looked straight into my eyes and said: 'It is unnatural, artificial and … American.' Luc believes AC actually makes you sick, and that we are supposed to feel the seasons. He thinks I want to control everything, but I personally think he is confusing control with comfort.

#keepyourcool

The buildings here in Paris are antique and so the solution is also antique – fans! Not electric ones. The kind you flutter in *Dangerous Liaisons*. Yes, the French will waft actual paper fans (or maybe a battery-powered one at a push) to get some kind of breeze on their faces. To be fair, the old stone buildings do stay a little cooler than an American office, where we would all be drowning in our own sweat in five minutes. But *really*? This is one area where the French are failing big time. At least get some large electric fans and make an effort. *#easybreezy*

If you haven't got time to find cool grass and a shady tree, then the only answer is to go to the chic shopping district with all the wonderful (and, more importantly, air-conditioned) designer stores. Here you can feel some blessed chill. And go shopping! *#winwin*

There are definitely times when it is a good idea to get out of the city altogether, sometimes to work, sometimes to get perspective and sometimes to avoid an awkward situation. What I've learned is that your awkward situation sometimes decides to come with you and that can make things even more difficult.

Or your awkward situation leaves you at the station and you have to go on your *voyage* alone.

The upside is a bit of *#metime* and *#girltime*. Because friends are the best.

My first trip out of Paris was unforgettable. When Camille invited me to her family château in Champagne, I had to say yes, and not just because it gave me a chance to win some new business for Savoir. I got to see first-hand the beautiful French countryside and the famous wine-producing region, with its serried rows of vines stretching away in velvety lines like a piece of green cord fabric.

If you are in France and can arrange a trip to the *campagne* (the countryside) then I highly recommend it as a way to refresh and appreciate another aspect of France. And if you happen to love wine, then a trip to a wine-growing region has all sorts of pleasures and experiences in store to enhance your *voyage*.

OH, CHÂTEAU!

While Mindy was at her friend Li's bachelorette party at La Nouvelle Eve, a cabaret in one of the oldest theaters in the Montmartre area, and getting sprayed with very expensive champagne, I was in the place those delicious bubbles are created.

Camille's family own the amazing Château de Lalisse, a gorgeous house that has been standing since the thirteenth century, but that was rebuilt in the nineteenth century in a classical style to look like everyone's idea of a fairy-tale French château. Despite being a castle full of antiques and gilt-edged portraits, it feels like a home, with a cosy and welcoming ambiance.

Although the scale is large, the pale beams and the white-painted walls give a stylish and manageable air to the space. In some rooms, the walls and floors are bare stone, but the white paint, washed linen fabrics and rush rugs soften the effect and add easy comfort. The keynote is the mix of old and new, simplicity and grandeur. That easy relationship makes an impressive building feel warm and approachable. Louise, Camille's mother, knows the effect of flowers and candles in providing glamour and a sense of luxury.

The outside is no less charming. The windows sport pale shutters, while pale-pink roses climb the walls and crumbling stone urns trail flowers. It's so picturesque. Imagine growing up in a place like this! Camille and her brothers must have had an idyllic childhood.

There is a touch of modern luxury in the sleek pool with its paved surround and beach loungers. Exactly what is needed in the heat of a French summer, when the crickets chirrup in the dark and the lavender releases its scent into the night air.

If you should happen to be lounging by the pool and a handsome young man offers you champagne from his own family vineyard, then I recommend that you accept… but make sure you check that he is exactly who you think he is. *#wrongbrother #embarrassing #sweetthough*

WHAT TO WEAR – CHÂTEAU CHIC

For a friendly family weekend, casual is the key. And you need to travel light. So your starting point can be a pair of jeans – practical and stylish, and easy to dress up or down.

When you're exploring, there is nothing more useful than jeans, a cosy sweater, and a beanie for wandering around in. I was traveling as light as possible since there was not much room for *bagages* in Camille's car, and I borrowed a pair of bright yellow boots so I could easily get around. Footwear like this is useful for cycling in particular, and also a help if you're planning to tour the area or travel to the market for those oh-so-important food supplies. Good hiking boots would be a great alternative. Anything sturdy, comfortable and waterproof will do.

For dinner, if it's just family, keep the informal note. You can stay in jeans but dress them up a little. A pink, cloud-soft, off-the-shoulder cashmere sweater with a red cami underneath (don't forget how well red and pink go together – if you paid attention in the fashion chapter, you'll know this!) is perfect, particularly with some sweet gold chains with disk pendants to add a touch of evening elegance.

A frilly blouse and a plaid jacket can give a more formal air to your trusty jeans, and will start getting you in the mood for your return to the city. A high-necked blouse can conceal a lot. *#hidemyhickey*

And, of course, you'll need your sunglasses. Not because you're embarrassed or anything. They're just useful.

For dinner, if it's just family, keep the informal note. You can stay in jeans but dress them up a little.

DON'T HAVE A CHÂTEAU TO VISIT? RECREATE THE STYLE OF DINNER AT CHÂTEAU DE LALISSE IN YOUR OWN HOME . . .

- **Pick up some old framed pictures at a flea market** – the older and dustier the better, as long as they look vintage. If you find old cutlery at the same time, then great! A mix of silverware looks fantastic.

- **Use real linen for your tablecloth, and for a French twist, put a lace or crocheted cloth over the top**. This will add to the sense of occasion. Add a folded linen napkin for each person.

- **Candles, candles and more candles.** Plain white in a mixture of candelabra and candlesticks. Turn off the lights and let the candles do their thing.

- **Put small sprays of roses on the table** in bud vases, one between every two people.

- **Mix your glassware with a selection of vintage engraved wine glasses.** Try different colors, sizes and textures as well – green for your white wine looks wonderful. Engraved coupes for champagne are perfect. For water, you can easily source cheap bistro-style glasses from lots of stores, including IKEA.

- **Put your bread in a basket in the middle of the table and serve unsalted butter, with sea salt in a little pot beside it.** Don't forget a pepper grinder; the French always require one.

- **Serve a French menu** of *coq au vin* (chicken in wine), grilled eggplant and a soufflé. In France, cheese comes before dessert, so serve your guests with French cheeses after the *coq*, and feel truly *sophistiquée*.

- **Drink Lalisse champagne,** I insist! It's delicious.

P.S. And please let women pour the wine. We can take a château vibe too far! It should be fun, not formal. #femmespourvins

If you're lucky enough to go to one of the many wine regions of France, then don't forget to take the opportunity to visit a vineyard or two. Wherever you go, you will see vineyards offering tours to visitors. You can usually tell this from a sign at the entrance that says '*Dégustation*' which literally means 'Tasting'. You go to the vineyard, tour the vines, the presses, the fermentation rooms and so on, and then end up in the cellar, where a bottle or two of the estate wine will be uncorked for you to try and, they hope, buy. And usually the more you try, the more in the mood to buy you become. It's another win for everyone!

Wine growers love sharing their knowledge and they will tell you exactly what kind of food goes best with their wines. You may be surprised by what they recommend.

CHAMPAGNE

Camille's (very intimidating – what is it with these older French women, they're all so formidable) mother clearly wanted me out of the house when we first arrived, and suggested I go on a tour of the Domaine de Lalisse's vineyard.

It was a good idea, not only because I wanted to get away from Gabriel, but also because I had to learn a little about their business. After all, I was there to find out more about representing their champagne. This led to the creation of Champère, the spraying champagne that used up the glut of grapes Camille's family needed to get rid of (thank you, Mindy, Li and the girls for that light-bulb moment!). And it was so interesting – especially when explained in Timothée's delicious accent! I'm glad to share a little with you so you know exactly what you're drinking when you sip those magical bubbles yourself.

I don't need to tell you that champagne is indelibly associated with all types of celebration – whatever the occasion, the pop and fizz of champagne adds joy and excitement.

Champagne has to come from the area of Champagne itself, which is called *appellation d'origine controlée* – or 'controlled naming of the origin'. This is so important to the French that they have created legal frameworks all over the world to protect the name Champagne. It was even part of the Treaty of Versailles after World War One! Not only that, but the grapes have to come from designated areas and the wine made to the exact specified method. They are tough about that. No cheating allowed.

Fizzy champagne was first created by mistake by Benedictine monks (who seemed to have created a lot of alcoholic drinks in their time, hence their reputation as the most fun-loving of all the monks). At first they thought the bubbles were a mistake and called their invention *le vin du diable*, the devil's wine, because of the way the corks popped out or the bottles exploded. Then they grew to like the bubbles.

A century or more later, bottles were developed that could withstand pressure, as well as corks that could be held in by little cages, and champagne became supercharged. Now there was a second fermentation *in the bottle*. Yeast and rock sugar were added to create the amazing fizz we know today.

Timothée explained that every bottle has to age for at least a year and a half, and during that time it is turned, a process called *remuage*. I am still thrilled by my title of *la reine de remueurs* – the queen of bottle turners – which I won by turning the most bottles the fastest in the cellars of the Lalisse vineyard! Timothée said it was down to my competitive American side, but I'll take that. I'm thinking of getting a button made. *#gotitgonnaflauntit*

Champagne is indelibly associated with all types of celebration.

MY FAVORITE CHAMPAGNES

Tattinger

I love Tattinger and it's Savoir's go-to champagne for any celebration. It's from a renowned family-owned house that has been producing its famous champagne for over a century. The deliciously dry bouquet has flavors of brioche, honeysuckle and pear. You can't go wrong with something so refined and so glamorous.

- **FAMOUS FANS:** *James Bond, Sylvie Grateau*

Dom Perignon

Dom Perignon was a Benedictine monk and winemaker. He improved the champagne method and introduced cork instead of wood to seal it. The label of Dom Perignon belongs to Moët and only started being sold last century. It is a single-vintage wine and if the grapes that year are not good enough, no wine is made, which increases its rarity. It tastes of smoke, biscuit and green apple.

- **FAMOUS FANS:** *Lady Gaga, Lenny Kravitz, hip-hop stars and rappers*

Veuve Clicquot

This is the grand old lady of champagne, known for its famous yellow label. On the cap is a portrait of the Widow (*veuve*, in French) Clicquot, after whom it's named. Only in her twenties at the time, Mme Clicquot took over the champagne house after her husband died in 1805. At a time when women were excluded from business, she made a huge success of it, and even created the first rosé champagne! Go, Widow! Her renowned champagne tastes of toast and biscuit with notes of citrus.

- **FAMOUS FANS:** *Tsars and Grand Dukes of Russia, Yayoi Kusama, polo players*

Pol Roger

The champagne of royal weddings, this graceful wine is fermented in cellars deeper than anywhere else in the area, which makes all the difference, I'm told. Famous

for its refinement and elegance, it has a world-class reputation as great champagne, boasting notes of stewed fruit.

- **FAMOUS FANS** *Winston Churchill, the British royal family*

Lalisse

Camille's family champagne, best served in a beautiful coupe. A delightful wine made from Chardonnay and Pinot Noir grapes, it has a biscuity taste with accents of grapefruit and peach, and too much can make you completely lose your inhibitions – especially when drinking by the pool with Timothée.

- **FAMOUS FANS:** *Pierre Cadault, Antoine Lambert*

THE
BEAUTIFUL
BEACH

Everyone loves the beach, but only in France can the seaside be so incredibly chic. Sylvie isn't particularly keen on 'damn beaches', as she calls them, but even she makes an exception for the pleasures of Saint-Tropez.

The French Riviera in the warm south, where Monaco nestles up to France, has been the playground of the rich and famous for years. Princes have flirted, movie stars have smoldered, millionaires have frittered fortunes, all while soaking up the sunshine, sailing in super yachts and whiling away the hours in luxury on the Côte d'Azur (the Blue Coast).

Can there be anywhere more glamorous than Cannes, home to the famous film festival? Just think of Brigitte Bardot, with her bee-stung lips, blonde hair and bikini, driving men wild. Sun, sex and red carpets are a heady mix.

When Mathieu suggested a weekend away in Saint-Tropez, I went because I liked him and because I needed to get my last night with Gabriel out of my mind. After all, it was supposed to be a farewell, not a hello. And he and Camille were over. I honestly thought it was a flash in the (omelette) pan, so I was totally shaken when I realized that Gabriel was sticking around after all, to go into business with Antoine. But it was too late to pull out of my fabulous break with Mathieu, not that I wanted to. I thought maybe we would make it work and I could forget that night of passion.

It looked like I was going to go to the coast on my own. Until Mindy and Camille joined me…then the fun and not-so-fun started. *#copinesenvacances*

Here are my top tips for a stay in Saint-Tropez…

Can there be anywhere more glamorous than Cannes, home to the famous film festival?

Sun, sex and
red carpets!

Coastal wear

- **A silk headscarf, silk-printed coat and driving gloves for your glamorous journey.** Wear with kitten-heeled sling-back pumps and statement shades to channel Eva Marie Saint or Grace Kelly in a Hitchcock movie.

- **Cute little strappy sundresses**, in vintage stripes or clashing florals, and a bucket hat for daytime. Wear with platform wedges or flats.

- **A bikini** – not black (unless you are Sylvie)! – and a colorful robe to wear over it.

- **A ruffled sundress and big straw hat** for an afternoon on fashion icon Grégory Duprée's yacht.

- **A sparkling, sequinned, fringed cocktail dress** for nights by the beach at the Laurent G club or by the pool at the Ragazzi House. Take a wrap and a biker jacket for when the night air gets cool. Match with some silver strappy heels.

- **Breton-stripe boat-neck tops and capri pants or shorts** will always shout timeless, sailor chic.

- **Sunglasses.** Of course.

- **Straw purses** – oversized and embellished, ideally.

- **Sneakers** for an emergency dawn dash to rescue a friend (Camille) in a church. *#unlikelybuttrue*

Don't forget a huge suitcase with Pierre Cadault's face on it to pack everything in.

WHERE TO STAY

A suite at the Grand-Hôtel du Cap-Ferrat could not be more amazing. It will come with complimentary champagne, chocolates and macarons and beautiful flowers everywhere, but you'll be obsessed with the glorious view with its sparkling azure sea and the magnificent yachts that glide across it. Although the suite is a wonderful home away from home, if you're like me, you'll want to be on the balcony, soaking it all in.

Or go to the roof of Club Dauphin, where there is a fabulous pool and where all the blues of sea and sky and water mingle into one delicious color. The beach loungers in blue and white stripes under chic white umbrellas provide shade and a contrast that pleases the eye. Nothing says seaside like blue and white.

And luckily the suite is big enough for you to share with your girlfriends if you find yourself on an impromptu girls' weekend, especially if one of them hooks up with a guy and stays elsewhere (looking at you again, Camille).

WHAT TO SEE

You must go the harbor and look at the fishing smacks, motorboats and super yachts, somehow coexisting side by side, crammed into their moorings or floating further out on the turquoise sea. The yachts are the stuff of dreams. Who knows which supermodel or pop star is stretching awake in a glamorous suite out there on the water? Or which Oscar winner or sports hero is soaking up rays on a deck? It's fun to wonder!

Walk through the cobble-lined streets, climb the narrow alleys with their shallow steps, admire the enchanting houses that come in exquisite shades of washed-out coral and faded orange, find quiet squares for a glass of wine and some lunch, and watch people playing *boules*, a French form of bowls, in the sandy patches in the middle. If you'd rather, you can stay in the bustling heart of town where the bistros and waterfront cafés are thronged and everyone is looking out for a famous face or two.

If you need some time to think and restore yourself, go up the road to Villefranche-sur-Mer and see the fabulous Chapelle Saint-Pierre, covered in the most amazing and graceful frescos by the poet Jean Cocteau. It's just the place to escape the bustle and contemplate the eternal in peace and tranquility.

FOOD

By the seaside you have to try out the seafood, of course! Eat oysters, or *huîtres* in French, served on ice. Squeeze lemon onto them or add a dash of Tabasco or a spoonful of shallot vinegar, and swig back each sea-flavored mouthful. Delicious! Perfect with ice-cold white wine. Or try a crisp salad full of fresh, ripe tomatoes and artichokes in herb vinaigrette. Just the thing in the heat of the day.

If you're walking by the harbor, get a refreshing *glace* or a sorbet – green apple or lemon is especially refreshing. Stop for a beer or a refreshing Aperol spritz. If you want a clear head, order a citron pressé. You'll get a glass of lemon juice accompanied by cute jugs of water and syrup so that you can mix your drink to your own taste. Perfect for a control freak like me.

Later in the evening, you can eat exquisitely cooked fish – the bream or red mullet caught that day – or feast on more shellfish, like langoustines, crab or lobster. This is best done sitting beachside at a table under a string of lights as the sun sinks into the sea.

Where to go. . .

- ### LAURENT G

This Riviera institution has been here for over twenty years, delighting customers with its position in a sweet and secluded cove. Tables line the waterfront, where bright clematis flowers flutter in the breeze. The blue sea on one side, and the hillside with hot pink bougainvillea flowers spilling down among the faded houses on the other makes for a delightful, picturesque contrast.

In the day, you can book paddleboards and enjoy a buffet on the beach. In the evening, things are more formal, and you'll be seated under the stars by the lapping ocean to feast on fresh seafood and divine salads. And if you have something to celebrate, don't forget to order the Champère. Remember: it's not for sipping, it's for spraying! Laurent is a charming host and I'm not saying that because he is married to my boss; he really is.

- ### RAGAZZI HOUSE

If you are lucky enough to get invited to this magnificent mansion, you have to go. It's dedicated to parties, with a huge pool, endless rooms and cool party areas, with lights, music and dancing. There are several bars, a bubble machine and a sound system that will keep you partying till the early hours. Enjoy the painted ceilings, terracotta-colored marble and impressive crystal chandeliers, along with the modern art (don't miss the Hockney in the billiard room). The atmosphere is super cool.

- ### CAFÉ SÉNÉQUIER

Mindy made us relive her childhood memories by visiting this Saint-Tropez landmark. She used to come here with her dad before he was the zipper king of China and she was just a kid, not an heiress-*cum*-failed Chinese popstar-*cum*-nanny-*cum*-drag *artiste-cum-chanteuse*. This bright-red bistro has provided delicious food and amazing views of the harbor since 1881. If you want to relive Mindy's Proustian moment too, order the *tarte tropézienne*, a brioche cake covered in melt-in-the-mouth pearl sugar – *délicieux!*

And if you're in the mood, you can stop for an Aperol or get on the yacht of any passing fashion designer who happens to have fooled you into joining his feud with Pierre Cadault. Up to you!

- ### LES CAVES DU ROY

I did not go to this legendary Saint-Tropez nightclub – after all, it was partly a work weekend for me – but if you get the chance, you must see it. Famous for the international stars, royalty, playboys and playgirls who throng it in high season to dance until the early hours, it has the joyful custom of playing a fanfare, strobing lights and setting off fireworks when someone orders a Methuselah of Louis Roederer Cristal champagne. If you knew how much they charge for that, you'd understand why they're celebrating.

Important French travel vocabulary

Train - train
Yacht - yacht
Cabin - cabine
Scooter - scooter
Vespa - Vespa
Bicycle - bicyclette

More important French travel vocabulary

Sleeping car - wagon-lit
Luggage - bagage
First class - première classe
Penthouse - penthouse
Grande suite - grande suite
Champagne - champagne
Chocolates - chocolats

HOW TO
TRAVEL

What are the best ways to see Paris and to escape the city? Here are some of my favorite ways to travel, inside the city and beyond. I have to be honest: I haven't ever caught a bus and I haven't used the *métro* since I got here. I'm lucky enough to live and work within walking distance of everywhere I need to be, and I love to walk so that's what I'll usually do. I will say, though, that I adore the *métro* signs. Unlike the ones in Chicago – which are very utilitarian – these are so chic! They are a lovely green color, with a fabulous font. Check them out when you're in Paris and you'll see what I mean.

RUNNING

I have seen so much of Paris's beauty by running through it. Of course, you need good footwear if you're going to run in the city, with all those hard surfaces. So make sure you invest in sneakers with lots of cushioning and change them every six months if you run a lot, and once a year if you run less.

My favorite running routes in Paris:

– Le Jardin du Luxembourg

This beautiful park is not far from my apartment. The Luxembourg Palace is now a government building and the gardens are renowned for their lawns, playgrounds, tree-lined avenues, and the octagonal pond known as the Grand Bassin, where model boats are sailed. There is the famous Medici fountain, and nearby are my favorite statues, a group of twenty-eight French queens and well-known women including, again, Sainte Geneviève, the patron saint of Paris. #womenofpower

Here you will see Parisian schoolchildren having fun in the playgrounds, people walking their pooches or reading on the benches, and lovers strolling together. It's a lovely place for a run, and there are plenty of water fountains if you feel dehydrated.

– The Seine

You can run for miles along the Seine, along the 'quais', crossing bridges and going back the other way whenever you want. You'll meet plenty of other Parisians doing the same thing, and although you'll sometimes have to wait at lights to cross a bridge, you'll be able to get a good steady pace. Some parts of the riverside have been pedestrianized, which makes running even easier. It's always uplifting to run through central Paris past some of its most famous landmarks.

– Canal Saint-Martin to the Parc de la Villette

The canal might not be as romantic in the day as it is in the evening, but it's still so pretty and a very straightforward place to run. Just stay beside the water! If you're lucky, they might have emptied the canal for its once-a-decade drain – everyone comes out to see what on earth has ended up in the bottom of it. #couldbegruesome Follow the cobbled curve of the canal as you take this easy-to-follow route north to the Parc. Explore the Parc de la Villette, or head back for the return leg. Once you get back, there are lots of excellent cafés for a post-run coffee and croissant.

– The Bois de Boulogne

This is Paris's second largest park and has three lakes, and wooded areas to run around, with plenty of maps to make sure you don't get lost. It's near the 16th arrondissement and has some lovely outdoor cafés and terrace restaurants, a riding school and a cute amusement park. It is also where the first manned balloon flight in history took place! When I run around this beautiful wood, I imagine that balloon lifting up into the air to the amazement of the watching citizens.

– Jardin des Plantes

Paris's beautiful botanical garden is full of thousands of specimens and home to the Natural History Museum. Come here for your fill of the natural world, a little bit of nature in this bustling city. You'll be breathing in all the wonderful oxygen exuded by the trees and plants, excellent for fighting the city's pollution, and the greenery will soothe the eyes as well.

BICYCLE

If you don't want to walk or run in Paris, you can always take a bicycle. Paris was one of the first cities to have a public bicycle rental system that allows you to pick up a bike from a docking station and leave it elsewhere in the city. You can rent normal or electric bikes for less than one hour or up to three days, and there are many cycle lanes and routes through the city. It's a wonderful way to get exercise, fresh air and see the sights at your leisure.

I loved cycling at Camille's château to the Champagne tour. I'd forgotten how much fun it is to feel the wind on your face and pedal along. Now I want to do it more often. There are 15,000 bicycles to rent in Paris so there really is no excuse. See you on a *vélo* very soon! Race ya...

#raceya

ELECTRIC SCOOTER

Electric scooters are the latest form of public transport in Paris. They're known as the *trottinettes*, which is such a sweet name, even though it sounds more like walking than scooting – but whatever, I've given up trying to understand this language, I've just given myself over to it. Unlike the bicycles, lots of different companies rent out scooters for different rates, so do your research to find the best deals (one even requires a driver's license). The thing to remember is you're not allowed to ride scooters on the sidewalk. It's illegal and you could be fined! But it is a fun way to zoom around this big city, or any of the cities in France, and save your feet from hours of walking.

VESPA

What could be more French than buzzing through the city on a Vespa? These mini motorbikes are just adorable and very easy to drive. In one of my more reckless moments, I borrowed a gorgeous promotional Vespa from outside Savoir and whizzed away, leaving Julien and Luc open-mouthed. They know how I feel about following the rules, so they understood that doing something so unexpected, and maybe even naughty, was completely out of character for me. But I loved it! I totally got why people love to zip through the narrow city streets on these machines. They're super fun and really an excellent way of getting around. I wanted to show Alfie that I am capable of being fun and spontaneous – so I obeyed my impulse and I'm glad I did. It was a blast!

For added Parisian chic, wear a custom Dior helmet. *#vavaVespa!*

What could be more French than buzzing through the city on a Vespa?

CAR

Perhaps the most awkward car journey I ever had was the journey to Camille's family home in her classic sports car. She told me what make it is, but I can't remember. It's red, I know that, and has very little space for luggage. I mean, one small case *each*. That's all it could take! The car was very pretty but I did have questions about the environmental aspect of a vehicle that old. But as usual, the French choose style over everything else and it is hard to blame them. The romance of the open road, the roar of the engine, the wind in your hair (wear sunglasses and a scarf, not just for the Hitchcock heroine vibe, but to protect yourself from that wind) is so seductive.

Camille's car also had no back seat to speak of, particularly once we'd crammed all our luggage in, and that meant I had to sit on Gabriel's knee all the way to Épernay, where Camille's château is situated. That's an hour and three quarters on the knee of my friend's boyfriend, the one I'd passionately kissed without my friend's knowledge.

So the whole thing became bittersweet because it was wonderful (and not a little exciting) to be so close to Gabriel and yet I couldn't stop feeling guilty about it, and so aware of his closeness, his hands, his shoulder, his legs, his breath on my neck … Oh, dear, I'm feeling jittery just thinking about it. What should have been a road trip blast became something else altogether. And the journey back, with that hickey on my neck, was worse … ugh. *#forgetforgetforget*

Château de Lalisse was the scene of my only Paris driving adventure. I can drive but I am not used to European stick shift. Read: I'd never driven it before. Add a man bleeding profusely after cutting off the tip of his own finger with a sword (and half fainting) – and another one, with said fingertip in an ice bucket, shouting, 'Drive, drive, get to the hospital quick!' – and you do not have the ideal conditions for your first automobile jaunt in the French countryside. How did we get to the hospital? I don't have a clue. But I didn't have to drive back, that was the main thing. And the finger was fine in the end, thank goodness, or it would have been something else to feel guilty for.

I can't see the point of having a car in Paris. Not only is the traffic bad enough without me adding to it, but I couldn't take the stress. That is why Uber was invented. Instant motor transport whenever you need and no worries about parking and insurance and road tax and all the other boring details that cars entail. You can also use the time in the Uber to check your social media feeds, do some posting, make a call and check your lipstick. Anything else just doesn't make sense!

LUXURY CAR 'MARQUES' THAT BRING THE ULTIMATE IN STYLE AND CLASS TO THE ROAD:

- **Bentley**
The famous luxury car of movie stars and soccer millionaires with distinct British style.

- **Daimler**
The choice of Queen Elizabeth II and high-class, high-net-worth magnates, sleek and classy.

- **Porsche**
The world's favorite jazzy sports car, with lots of celebrity fans, including Mariah Carey, Emma Raducanu, and Keanu Reeves, who once owned forty-six at the same time! *#garagespace?*

- **Ferrari**
The ultimate in classic chic, this famous speedster was owned both by John Lennon and Elvis Presley. *#rockitout*

- **Lamborghini**
The luxury car beloved of playboys and the offspring of billionaires. Often in striking colors – bespoke shades proclaim ultra wealth! Choice of Kim Kardashian and Nicki Minaj.

Bentley

Porsche

I have to admit that I am very lucky. My job working with luxury brands means that I get to travel in some beautiful cars. I will never forget the chauffeur-driven Bentley that took me from the station to my hotel on the Riviera, a ride of dreams in a gorgeous car trimmed in luxurious padded white leather (okay, full disclosure: it was in Mathieu's name and because he'd left me at the station at the Gare de Lyon, I felt a little guilty taking advantage of it – but what can an American girl do?). It glided along the famous hairpin bends on the way to the coast, taking every turn with grace, and I felt like a movie star. Bentley is one of the great luxury *marques* and it was a privilege to enjoy such a journey all to myself. The conscience-easing aspect is that the newer cars are the most environmentally friendly of all. Obviously no car is perfect, but small steps make a difference. If you ever get the opportunity to be driven in a car like that, don't hesitate! *#smalltowngirl #livingmydream*

TRAIN

Train travel is perhaps the most civilized there is. It has an old-world feel that everything else lacks, and can provide the most extraordinary sense of luxury, as though you are traveling in a moving hotel. The Belmond Pullman is the last word in luxury train travel. This train is the famous Orient Express, calling at London, Paris and Venice, and if you possibly can, you must travel aboard. Every detail is sublime, from the polished inlaid wood to the beautifully upholstered seats. The perfection of every last element is just amazing.

On the Pullman, you'll find restaurant cars, each one themed to a different color and style, where delicious à la carte meals are served accompanied by the finest wines. There's even a carriage devoted entirely to a wonderful bar, where you can sit on velvet banquettes and listen to a pianist playing Cole Porter and Irving Berlin while you sip a martini, perfectly mixed by your white-coated barman and served on tray by a waiter. Your cabin miraculously transforms into a cute sleeping berth, with elegantly made bunk beds so that you sleep in comfort as the train rolls on through the night. Your steward is in the Pullman livery, complete with hat and gloves. It's like traveling with F. Scott Fitzgerald and Zelda in the golden age of luxury.

Mathieu had booked our *wagon-lit* (sleeping car) for the journey to the coast, but as you know, I ended up having it to myself. If you can't quite manage this level of luxury – and I only could thanks to Mathieu – you can still travel by train. It's the best way to make a long journey, in my opinion. The TGV (*train grande vitesse*, the superfast train) gets you all over France in air-conditioned comfort.

Travel-wear essentials:

- **An easy-to-carry backpack.**

- **Headphones and chargers.**

- **A relaxing, sleep-promoting playlist** – to drown out the noise of travel or other passengers.

- **An eye mask** – silk is best, to protect your lashes.

- **A neck pillow** – there are fabulous structured scarves that support your neck without looking like you're wearing a lifesaver around it. If you don't want a painful crick and don't want to use airline pillows, then one of these is easy to pack and useful.

- **Moisturizing cream and lip balm** – always keep moisturized, especially at high altitude.

- **Foldable water bottle** – a reusable and convenient way to carry water. You can easily fold it up when not in use, and fill it when you have the opportunity. Don't forget to stay hydrated! Avoid too much alcohol and caffeine on planes.

- **Hand sanitizer and tissues** – just because. Public bathrooms are not always the most lovely places in the world. That's all.

Travel is a wonderful, modern blessing and I've been lucky enough to have some amazing experiences.

My favorite journey is just walking through the city, finding new nooks and crannies I didn't already know about. This city keeps surprising me. Walking is fun and uplifting, and slows your pace so that you can really see what's around you. When the surroundings are as beautiful as they are in Paris, that's quite a gift. So, if you can, put on your walking shoes and set out.

And you know what? Look up. Look at the sky, the top of the buildings, the magnificent roofs and everything you don't see at eye level. A whole new world will open up to you.

I'm so grateful for this journey that brought me to Paris. Who knows what adventures are next? Don't stop me now!

Travel is a wonderful, modern blessing and I've been lucky enough to have some amazing experiences.

EMILY'S 'LOST IN TRANSLATION' PARIS

Chapter 7

It's no secret that I didn't speak French when I arrived in Paris. Okay, I still don't speak French, but I can understand a lot more and even make myself understood from time to time.

It took a while even to master the basics. The whole masculine/feminine thing is very confusing. In English, we say 'a' or 'the', but in French, they have one word for masculine and another for feminine – so *un* or *une* for 'a', and *le* and *la* for 'the' – and a whole host of other things follow on from this, in terms of everything agreeing and matching up. You are actually supposed to remember whether every noun in French is masculine or feminine! How do they do that?

When I went to the bakery, it really mattered that I said *un pain au chocolat* not *une*. And it was *une bonne journeé*, not *un bon journé*. French is a language that hasn't got the non-binary memo. But I used this to my advantage when my post about the vagina being masculine in French went viral. It traveled all the way to Brigitte Macron at the Élysée Palace! That was one of my first real triumphs at Savoir.

Even when you begin to use the right words, or at least understand them, it doesn't follow that you've got the right meaning. After living here for a while, I sometimes feel stupid in two languages, not one. But I think, gradually, I'm beginning to find my way around this extraordinary French tongue. *#thatisnotadoubleentendre #ohIjustspokeFrench!*

My American friend Judith Robertson remarked that the French 'r' sound doesn't really exist, along with a whole load of completely soundless letters (X? S? T? Why are they silent? They are like the noisiest letters in the alphabet!). It's as though 'r' can't be bothered to come out of the mouth but stays lodged in the throat somewhere. A bit like the speaker wants to spit something out. Sounds bad, but you get used to it.

But for all of that, French is also the most romantic language in the world. Honestly, until a man has murmured in French while he's making love to you, you have *no idea* … well, I guess you can imagine. *#sigh #beautifulnight*

FALSE FRIENDS OR 'FAUX AMIS'

Beware of words that sound the same but don't mean the same as English. Mindy explained this to me after I asked for a croissant with *preservatif*. I thought I was asking for jam. I was actually asking for a condom.

I told Antoine that I was very *excitée* about being at the shoot for the De l'Heure commercial. And I had just told him that I was horny. That, of course, was the last thing I wanted to say to him, and I certainly didn't want to imply such a thing in front of Sylvie. That was a box of frogs I didn't want to open.

Mindy told me a few others to beware of:

- *Crayon* is a pencil
- *Médicin* is a doctor
- *Blessé* doesn't mean blessed, it means hurt
- Your *bras* is your arm
- A *raisin* means a grape
- A *coin* is a corner
- A *location* is a rental, not a place
- A *blanquette* is a veal stew
- A *cave* is a cellar
- *Chance* means luck

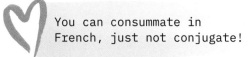

Mindy's Wisdom

You can consummate in French, just not conjugate!

I could go on; there are so many. You will only learn through experience. But let me warn you about one very important difference.

In France, *collège* means high school. And their word for college is *université*.

I will let that sink in.

Can you see how confusing that could be?

It's no wonder that I ended up in bed with Timothée, thinking he was Camille's older brother. I will certainly never forget that particular *faux ami*.

Faux Ami?

One word that is certainly not a false friend is *quarantine*. As I discovered when Sylvie quarantined me from luxury brands for offending Pierre Cadault, it means the same thing in English.

Thank goodness I managed to win back Pierre as a client and reposition him in modern fashion with my best brainwave of all: to have him hijack Grey Space in an even bigger, better and splashier way than they hijacked me! *#stillwashinggraypaintoutofmyhair*

Sylvie's Wisdom

You can't talk your way out of this one, Emily. You don't have the 'vocabulaire'

I'm trying to improve. I'm going to French class, and I'm doing my best. Here are some things I've picked up along the way.

- **_Non_**
  You'll hear this a lot. It can break a girl's spirit unless she's determined not to take _non_ for an answer!

- **_Pas possible_ – not possible**
  This is delivered without apology and is basically no – with extra 'no' emphasis. It means no, case closed, don't bother asking anymore, I'm not interested, it's finished, goodbye. This is said particularly by people whose job it is to help you, like a plumber.

- **_Exactement_ – exactly**
  This ought to be a signal of agreement. Exactly! Yes! And it often is. But when Sylvie says it, she really means to imply that I'm so incredibly slow that I have only just caught up with what was clear to everyone else about ten minutes ago. So it's a very clever veiled insult – in Sylvie's mouth, at least.

- **_C'est la vie_ – that's life**
  I used to think that this was quite a charming expression of resignation and Gallic shrugging, delivered with a smile. But now I have the distinct impression that it is another way of saying _deal with it, baby_! That's how it comes across when my work colleagues say it to me, in any case.

- **_Désolé_ – sorry**
  Pronounced 'desolay' like 'desolated', it's supposed to mean 'sorry', but when it's uttered by Sylvie with a sarcastic look on her face, it can often sound much more like 'not sorry one bit'. I find I'm the one saying it most of the time, but the difference is that I really mean it!

- **_C'est normal_ – it's normal**
  Whenever you point out how strange things are in France, they shrug and say _c'est normal_. Guys, IT'S NOT NORMAL. Otherwise it would not be so confusing. _#cestobvious_

- **_Voilà_ – there it is**
  Another false friend. I thought it was a positive thing – 'look at this brilliant thing', or 'here is the answer!' – but no, it seems to usually mean that I was too dumb to see what everyone else could. Then again, every now and then, I have the satisfaction of being able to say _voilà_ myself! And I must admit it feels good, so I can't really blame anyone else for doing the same.

- ***Courage* – be brave/good luck**
  I need this. I have to say it to myself every day on the way into the office. *Courage*, Emily! Today might be better than yesterday. Maybe.

- ***Terminé* – finished**
  This can mean a relationship broken up, and it can mean you're fired. Sometimes it means both on the same day, and that is one bad day.

- ***Enchanté* - enchanted**
  This is what French people say when they're introduced to one another, and I'll say it again, I love it. The old-world charm is so seductive.

- ***Génial* – cool, great**
  This word is so French; they are always saying things are *génial* and when they do, you can relax, everything is fine, no one is cross with you, wants to fire you, or any of that – thank goodness!

- ***Joyeux anniversaire* – happy birthday**
  This can be sung in French to the same tune as our 'Happy Birthday', and guess what? It sounds just as wonderful sung by French friends as it does at home.

- ***Pardon* – excuse me**
  I need this word a lot; somehow I'm always treading on toes and upsetting people, even when I mean well. It's had a lot more use than I hoped – but people generally forgive me. #intheend

- ***Santé* – good health**
  Pronounce this at the end of toasts as you clink glasses, and then sip your wine, confident that all this French food and drink isn't doing you any harm at all.

- ***Très bien* – very good**
  An excellent catch-all response, especially when someone you have mortally offended by sleeping with their boyfriend – even though you thought they'd broken up – asks you to conduct a meeting in French. *Merci*, Camille …

- ***Répétez, s'il vous plait* – come again?**
  Literally, 'please repeat'. If you're slow of understanding in French, you will need this phrase. Though you might not particularly want to hear what your ex-best friend (Camille) has to say to you – not twice, at least. Even if you can't understand it. #Igotthegist

- ***Le poireau* – a leek**
  Something complex, mysterious and versatile. Something subtle, elusive and misunderstood. Sweet but earthy, deserving of international recognition. A little like me, I like to think. And a chance to redeem myself, according to Sylvie.

You can probably tell by this that I'm in no way equipped to tell you how to speak French, but I hope these little pointers prove useful. If you ever get stuck, though, and there isn't a friendly English speaker in the room, never forget: Google Translate is very, very helpful.

Pierre's Wisdom

You can speak all the badly
accented French you like, but
you'll never understand me and
I'll never understand you

DIFFERENT STROKES

As an American who'd never been abroad, I found so much about life in Paris –
beyond just the language – completely bewildering. They just don't follow the same
rules and customs as we do, even though outwardly so much is the same. It can take
a while to get used to new ways of doing things. Some I will never understand and
others I learned to come to terms with.

- **Merde**
  People let their dogs poop on the sidewalk and don't pick it up! Unbelievable.
  I guess they can't smell it because they're usually smoking. But it is no joke
  finding you've just landed your boot or shoe into another steaming pile, courtesy
  of someone's prized pet. It just doesn't seem to bother anyone. The streets are
  spray-cleaned most mornings, so at least you don't have to live with it for long.

  Even weirder is that there are urinals in the street. Yes. In the street. Men walk
  up, unzip and pee right there. In a nod to modesty, the urinals have high sides
  so you don't get a profile view, but you can still hear the stream. They call it a
  pissoir. I can't even say that in polite company!

- **Smoking**
  The fact that smoking kills you seems to have bypassed Parisians. People smoke
  all the time. They smoke outside the gym, for crying out loud! Sylvie smokes in
  the office, which I thought was illegal, but perhaps she thinks it keeps her thin.
  My feeling is that cancer is a side effect I'd rather avoid. But then, I like to eat my
  calories and Sylvie likes to drink hers. To each her own. Even Gabriel smokes,
  which I think is a shame, but I hope he'll give it up before too long.

- **Reversing dates**
  The French put the day and month the wrong way around. When I went to
  book a table at the Michelin-starred Le Grand Véfour, one of the most famous
  and exclusive restaurants in Paris, for the dinner with Randy Zimmer, I spent
  ages making sure I could grab one of the cancellations. When I managed it,
  I was thrilled! But I had booked for November 8th instead of August 11th. ☹
  That's because the French follow the European style of putting the day before
  the month – 11/8 means the 11th of August. How confusing is that?!

The fact that smoking kills you seems to have bypassed Parisians. People smoke all the time.

- **Floor numbers**

Calling the first floor the ground floor makes life needlessly complicated and I think we should all sort this one out and agree to do it the American way. Also, put elevators into old buildings if at all possible, especially if you happen to have a lot of suitcases or packages arriving from America, or a roommate who needs one to get all her possessions into your little *chambre de bonne*. *#ImtalkingaboutyouMindy*

- **As Mindy says, the customer is never right**

  Here, the waiting staff hold all the power and the chef's word is law. If you don't like your steak bloody, then you might not get anything at all. The chef is quite likely to come out and challenge you if you ask for your food the way you like it. But then, if the chef is Gabriel, you will quickly backtrack, try the food and realize that you have just eaten something incredible. So I'm not saying it's all bad, it is just a very different way of doing things. And the staff can be pretty short if they decide, for whatever reason, that they don't like you, or they are too busy to deal with you. *#youstilltipthough*

- **Washing dishes**

  The French do wash dishes, but they have an exception: they don't clean their pans. Soap is no good, apparently, for the kind of cast-iron pans they use for omelettes. They simply wipe them out and use them again like that. As Gabriel puts it, 'We never clean, we let things ... season.' I had eaten the omelette – and knew how delicious it was – before I learned this, or I might have felt differently, but how can I say it's a bad thing when the food tastes so good? I promised Gabriel that I would never wash his pan, and I won't. *#season*

- **French endings**

  The French look down on American movies – at least, that's what Luc and Julien told me. They said that American endings give you hope, as though that is a bad thing. Luc said he wants to see the hero tortured for love and maybe lose a limb, and the heroine become a lesbian, because that happens in real life pretty often, apparently. They think French endings are tragic and therefore more realistic.

  But I think we need a little escapism sometimes, and to be cheered up. Luc seems to think that being depressed makes us feel better about our own lives. But then, he's the kind of guy who likes to contemplate death on his birthday and ponder the long, cold nothingness of eternity, so should we listen to him? I'm not sure ... *#gethappy*

- **Home Sweet Château**

  I thought that Louise would be dying to show me all around her beautiful home. I know Americans would be leading the way on a tour in a heartbeat if they had such a great place to live. But she was completely baffled when I suggested it. She seemed to think it was rude and completely out of the ordinary to show someone your house. Luckily Camille was there to smooth it all out and make peace. I got to see the vineyard and the pool instead, and maybe more of Gérard than I would have wanted.

  In France, you can't see someone's upstairs but you are very much permitted to see their downstairs. *#andhow*

- ***Smiling***

  Apparently you're not allowed to smile in Paris unless you are so happy you can't help it. And if you do smile too much, they just think you're dumb. I mean – *what?*

- ***There is an 'i' in team***

  Because while there isn't one in English, there is one in *équipe*, the French word for team, so apparently my ideas of working together don't make any sense here. Or so Sylvie says. *#butIwanttobeonherteam*

- ***Don't touch the wine bottle (apparently)***

  If you're a woman it's not the done thing. I'll have another glass while you're at it, *merci.*

- ***The city is OLD***

  Paris is ancient in a way that is completely unfamiliar to me. Gabriel was not joking when he said that the plumbing in our building was five hundred years old. That means the system collapses all the time and is not easy to mend. Similarly, the electrical systems are also unreliable. Okay, not quite five hundred years old, but at least a century in some cases. That means you can easily blow a fuse and plunge your apartment into darkness. Your whole building, even. Most of your street, in fact. If you plug in something that requires a lot of … er … power, be warned. *#goodvibrations*

FOOD IS A UNIVERSAL LANGUAGE

When we're eating, we don't need words to unite us in mutual pleasure of taste and experience.

We all know that France and food go together like Bogart and Bacall – you can't think of one without the other. Just watch *Ratatouille*, if you haven't already, and you'll see what I mean. And this is one area where the Americans are in awe of the French. Like the French, we love food, and the whole of Paris is a temple to fine dining of a sort that we don't come across as often back home. No wonder people make their way here from all over the world to sample French cuisine.

Food is a religion in Paris, and so much of the city is devoted to the pleasure of eating. If its citizens aren't thinking about sex, they're thinking about their stomachs. Even someone like Sylvie, who hardly eats at all, makes sure that when she does indulge herself, it's with something amazing. *#bonappetit*

There are some foods for which the French don't appear to have any words at all. Fudge, for example. They are also inexplicably opposed to Chicago's signature deep-dish pizza. The fact it lasts six months is apparently a downside in France, not a convenience.

Mindy's Wisdom

In Paris, everyone is serious about dinner

France is the home of *gastronomie* and the language of cookery is French. The highest honors awarded to chefs – le Cordon Bleu (the Blue Ribbon) and Michelin stars – are based in France. A background in French classic cookery is still considered a vital element of any chef's training, and French influence pervades most professional cooking.

The great nineteenth- and early twentieth-century chef Auguste Escoffier is regarded as one of the first people to codify haute cuisine (high or fine cookery), or classic French cooking and its techniques and terms. He came up with the *brigade de cuisine*, still used in professional restaurant kitchens. He went into business with César Ritz, and created the ultimate in luxury dining at the finest hotels that still resounds today.

Watch:

Ratatouille

Julie and Julia

Chocolat

Haute Cuisine

Read:

Down and Out in Paris and London by George Orwell

Kitchen Confidential by Anthony Bourdain

A Taste of Paris by David Downie

EATING IN PARIS

Paris is bursting with wonderful food shops and markets. As I mentioned before, don't forget to visit the Grande Épicerie de Paris, the incredible food hall at Le Bon Marché department store, to see a display of produce laid out like a work of art. It's a shrine to food. Paris is crammed with great places to eat – cafés, bistros, restaurants and street food vendors. There are American diners and British pubs as well, if you're missing home as much as Alfie does.

If you want to eat like a Parisian, it's easy!

Mindy's Wisdom

♡ Sancerre is a breakfast wine

'LE PETIT DÉJEUNER' – BREAKFAST

Forget healthy breakfasts, the French prefer speed – a croissant and coffee on the run. A plain croissant takes on a whole new character when dipped into a frothy milky coffee. The key is to have just one, and then save yourself for the first real meal of the day.

There are now more breakfast options in Paris, and people also take out their coffees rather than drink them standing up at a bar or sitting at a table on the street, though you will, of course, still find Parisians doing this.

These days there are plenty of choices you'll be familiar with: juices, smoothies, granolas, yogurt… and there are more brunch options too. The French more or less invented those delicious brunch meals we love so much: eggs Benedict, eggs Royale, and so on, as well as pancakes, porridge, açai bowls and Bircher muesli. They are not so good at bacon, and tend to produce a kind of fried ham. But nobody's perfect! You could just have breakfast *à la* Sylvie – black coffee and a cigarette – but I don't recommend it.

'DÉJEUNER' – LUNCH

The first proper meal of the day is lunch. It's not quite as serious as dinner, but it's getting there (and on a really stressful day, you'll have a glass of wine before noon, but that's okay. *#nojudgment*).

The first time I saw everyone from my office having lunch at the Bistro Valois – without me, I might add, having told me they were otherwise engaged – I couldn't believe my eyes. Not only were they upending their second or even third empty wine bottle into the ice bucket (a signal to the waiter that they can remove it and, very likely, bring another), but also, they were all smoking. And it was barely two o'clock. This is not in the least unusual. In Paris, everyone understands the necessity of a well-deserved lunch break, even if they only got into the office at 11.30. After all, how can someone work on less than a two-course meal and several glasses of invigorating wine? *#sarcasticmoi?*

If you're not invited, then a great lunch option is to take a baguette and some cheese and *jambon* (ham) into the Jardin du Palais-Royal and find a quiet bench, where you look forward to eating it until a couple of kids come and knock it out of your hand.

Mindy's Wisdom

♡ Drink away your guilt

A CAFÉ IN PARIS

Once you see your first proper Paris café, you know you've arrived in this famous city. You'll find dozens, and often very similar ones: intimate dining areas with small tables and chairs (sometimes in the classic green and white cane) outside facing the street, and white-aproned servers gliding between them bearing trays of drinks to the customers. Take a table and wait.

I love to go to Le Flore en l'Île and take one of the steel-topped tables, each with a pair of cane chairs, so I can gaze out over the Seine to where I can see the rotunda of the Panthéon rising near my little home. The bridges stretch away along the river. To my right, Notre-Dame rises up, and large *bateaux* float away down the water. The waiter arrives. He's not exactly chirpy but he takes my order for a *café crème*. The waiter returns quickly with my coffee and my bill on a saucer. Around me, people come and go, ordering wine or beer, sometimes a toasted sandwich and *frites* or a salad. The waiter comes back for my money, and I tip him a euro, then finish my coffee at leisure before heading off to meet Mindy for some shopping. Then we'll have a glass of wine together at our favorite café near my apartment, the Café de la Nouvelle Mairie. It has a handy view of Gabriel's restaurant, but that's not why I like it.

'LE DINER' – DINNER

This is the most exciting meal of the day for Parisians. Now the restaurants have opened, the lights are on, and the diners arrive for the serious matter of their dinner. First the *entrées*, the starters – not the main course as we understand *entrée* to mean back home in the US. Try a French classic like French onion soup, or a *céleri rémoulade* (a delicious salad of chopped celeriac in a mustard and mayonnaise dressing) or, if you're feeling brave, some snails in garlic butter.

Now the *plat principal* – the main course. You could have *poisson* – fish. Try a classic fish stew, called a *bouillabaisse*, full of delicious fish and seafood. Or go for the *viande* – the meat. France is famous for *steak frites*, of course, but you mustn't play it too safe.

Try your steak raw, maybe? *Steak tartare* is served with little dressings for you to mix into raw chopped steak, including a raw egg. I promise, it's much nicer than it sounds. Some chefs from Normandy can even make tripe taste delicious. So be adventurous!

(Hint: there is a limit. Never order the *ris de veau* – Mindy says it might be balls or brain, but it tastes like ass.)

Now it's time for dessert. Parisians do not eat huge desserts. They are, of course, delicious, but usually pretty small (desserts, not Parisians). In a typical restaurant, like a brasserie, you'll find *crème caramel*, *crème brûlée* (literally burned cream, but that sounds gross, and it's much nicer than that, with sugar forming a delicious crispy surface), a slice of tart with *crème anglaise* and glazed fruit, a soufflé, or something very rich and chocolatey.

Light and elegant is usually the best choice. One of my favorites is *îles flottantes* (floating islands), balls of meringue floating in a sea of vanilla sauce. It's mind-blowing, like eating sweet air. At a dinner party, the hostess will often provide a very good fruit tart from a local patisserie.

By the way, *crème brûlée* is great for releasing tension. Just ask Pierre Cadault, who soothes a raging heart by cracking the crisp toffee top with the back of a spoon. I've tried it, and it's very satisfying.

Gabriel's Wisdom

Keep the heat low, and take it slow

THE FRENCH CLASSIC – 'L'OMELETTE'

When all my stuff arrived from America, I was heartbroken that my jars of Trader Joe's organic unsalted chunky peanut butter had smashed. So Gabriel cooked me an omelette. The most amazing thing I've ever tasted! So simple and so incredibly delicious. It is a French classic that I cannot make as well as Gabriel, but now that I have his pan, I'm going to learn because I had no idea that eggs, butter, herbs and seasoning could taste so amazing... If you get the chance, pop into Chez Lavaux and order it. You won't be disappointed.

PERFECT BIRTHDAY PARTY DINNER

- Go shopping with Gabriel.

- Cook roast chicken with the freshest vegetables and make a delicious salad.

- Obey Gabriel and don't get in the way of your ingredients.

- Have a romantic setting in a Paris square, with candles and flowers.

- Serve plenty of wine.

- Get Gabriel to make your birthday cake – chocolate with three layers of Belgian chocolate mousse and sea salt. *Sublime.*

- Toast with Château de Lalisse champagne.

- Don't let your friend find out that you slept with her boyfriend. It puts a dampener on the whole thing.

FOOD SHOPPING

Paris has amazing food markets. If you're in the city, you must visit one of these incredible places, full of stalls selling the most wonderful produce. You'll find everything you could want – breads, cheeses, meat, fish and seafood, vegetables, salad…it's all there, fresh and delicious…

– Le Marché des Enfants Rouges, Le Marais

Paris's food market recommended to me by Camille. You can buy your produce here, but also stop at one of the interesting food stalls to have lunch. The market is named after an orphanage, which kind of melts the heart…

– Marché Bastille

Twice a week you'll find really good vegetables, cheeses, chicken and fish for sale in this market. The dried meats are also notable.

– Marché Président-Wilson

This fabulous market offers the best of Parisian *gastronomie*, plus some awesome street food to tempt and delight. And, of course, it's named after the president who helped France win World War One, so going there is simply a patriotic duty.

– Marché Monge

Super high quality, a wonderful, artisan market full of wonderful, rustic foods. It's expensive, but so pretty it's worth it! *#stylefirst*

Useful French phrases

Can you explain that more slowly?
Pouvez-vous expliquer ça plus lentement?

Why am I still on beginner-level French?
Pourquoi je n'ai pas progressé?

Great to meet you!
Enchantée.

That makes zero sense
Ça n'a pas de sens.

My fault!
C'est ma faute!

But why? I don't understand!
Mais pourquoi? Je ne comprends pas!

Oh my God, that's delicious
Oh mon dieu, c'est délicieux.

Please, let me eat that again
Je peux en avoir encore?

Don't stop, Gabriel . . .
Continues, Gabriel . . .

Yes, just like that
Oui, comme ça.

Oh la la
Ooh là là

EMILY'S LIFE LESSONS

Chapter 8

My horizons have expanded in so many directions since I came to live and work in Paris. It was supposed to be a year. Now I don't know. I'm still deciding what I want my future to look like. Of course I miss home, I miss my family and all my great friends. But they will still be there, and I may never get this amazing chance again.

I feel like I'm just beginning to find my feet here and maybe it's too soon to go back. I have a strong inner sense that there is even more to learn and more fun to be had.

#lifeisamazing

I think I'm a different Emily from the girl who turned up fresh off the plane, excited but apprehensive. I hid a lot of my fears with a big smile and a confident demeanor, but I was afraid. I'm proud that I conquered that fear and set about tackling my new life, even if I made lots of mistakes along the way. I should definitely have learned more about Paris before I came, instead of trying to learn French on the plane. My motto was 'fake it till you make it' and that is great in some ways. Sometimes you have to act confident to be confident, but you also need to put the work in – do your research, keep learning. Things got better when I started to do that.

Since then, my confidence has grown. I've learned to trust my instincts and to speak up. I've learned to take on people who try to bring me down. That whole *La Plouc* thing was actually a lot like bullying, and I wouldn't let it pass. Now those bullies respect me, and they're my friends.

I've learned to value myself first, and that way it's a lot easier to ask other people to value you. When Doug wanted me to give up on this fabulous opportunity and go home, I knew that the relationship was no good. He didn't really want what was best for me. And with Thomas – once I realized he looked down on me, I knew we weren't compatible.

I've learned you can make new friends anywhere you go. It was luck that brought Mindy to me, but we instantly clicked, so I went for it. The same with Camille. When she stepped in to help me buy roses and then invited me to her gallery, I knew she had a kind and friendly heart, and I'm so glad I accepted her invite. She and Mindy brought warmth, support and fun into my life when I badly needed it. I hope I've done the same for them too.

To build a brand, you must create meaningful social engagement.

Which is a little like life, when you think about it.

Luc's Wisdom

You can never escape life!

I've learned that it's okay to make mistakes but you also have to own them, and try to fix them. When I offended Pierre, I knew I had to put it right. And when Camille found out about me and Gabriel, I couldn't be happy until I'd apologized and made it right with her. I'm still learning, of course, but I've accepted that I'm not perfect, and I always endeavor to see where I've gone wrong and do better next time.

I've learned to have fun. It has come as a surprise to me, but life doesn't have to be tidy, and stored in little containers, and governed by rules. You can break rules, challenge yourself, get out of your comfort zone, live a little and be messy. Your life and your heart won't always go in the directions you want them to. Who wants to fall in love with their friend's boyfriend? What happens when you do? What if you can't make yourself stop loving him, and what happens if he starts to love you?

It would be so easy if things were nice and neat, but they're not. Sometimes you have to accept that.

For months, I thought Sylvie hated me and that she didn't value my work. I also thought that my way – the American way – was best. I can't believe I passed the corporate commandments around the office and actually thought they should all do as I wanted.

Now Sylvie has left Savoir – something I never expected – and wants me to join her. And I'm thinking that maybe Madeline has got it all wrong. We should tear up those corporate commandments after all, because maybe all the commanding we're doing is crushing people instead of setting them free to do what we actually want them to do – make the magic happen.

I'm excited about the future, but worried too, in case I make the wrong choice. But that's okay. I've learned to think a bit more before I act.

Most of all, I have learned that I can have it all. And you know what?

I deserve it. And so do you.

Emily

♡ xoxo

Be positive

Work hard

Make mistakes

Own your mistakes

Value yourself

Speak up!

Be excited by life

Have fun

Get messy

Keep learning

Good luck, biche!

Voracious / Little, Brown and Company
Hachette Book Group
1290 Avenue of the Americas, New York, NY 10104
voraciousbooks.com

First Edition: October 2022

Voracious is an imprint of Little, Brown and Company, a division of Hachette Book Group, Inc.
The Voracious name and logo are trademarks of Hachette Book Group, Inc.

The publisher is not responsible for websites (or their content) that are not owned by the publisher.

The Hachette Speakers Bureau provides a wide range of authors for speaking events.
To find out more, go to hachettespeakersbureau.com or call (866) 376-6591.

Written by Kirsty Crawford
Artwork by Jacqueline Bissett
Design by Nikki Dupin / Studio Nic & Lou

All photos courtesy of Viacom International Inc. except for the following:
p.11 Alexandre Lallemand / Unsplash, Alex Williams / Unsplash; p.13 Petr Kovalenkov / Shutterstock; p.25 Sebastien Gabriel / Unsplash; p.49 Michael Fousert / Unsplash, Joseph Ndungu / Unsplash; p.55 Amersfoort 001 / Unsplash; p.61 Anthony Delanoix / Unsplash; p.63 Leonard Cotte / Unsplash, Christian Alder / Unsplash, Frédéric Soltan / Corbis News / Getty Images; p.77 Bettman / Getty Images; p.78 Frederic Reglain / Alamy Stock Photo, Mark Piasecki / Getty Images News / Getty Images; p.84 Fred Nassar / Unsplash; p.91 Big Dodzy / Unsplash, Mika Baumeister / Unsplash; p.95 gabriel12 / Shutterstock; p.101 Edward Berthelot / Getty Images Entertainment, Catarina Belova / Shutterstock; p.123 Muhammed Abiodun / Unsplash; p.125 Lucy Joy / Unsplash; p.128 Kiev.Victor / Shutterstock, alarico / Shutterstock; p.135 Alexander / Unsplash; p.137 STF / AFP / Getty Images, John Kellerman / Alamy Stock Photo, Barbara Alper / Archive Photos / Getty Images; p.139 AA World Travel Library / Alamy Stock Photo, Kilyan Sockalin / Unsplash, iFocus / Shutterstock, LMPC / Getty Images; p.140 Pictorial Press Ltd / Alamy Stock Photo, LMPC / Getty Images, Album / Alamy Stock Photo; p.151 javarman / Shutterstock; p.159 golibo / iStock, Archivio Cameraphoto Epoche / Hulton Archive / Getty Images; p.167 Yannick Van Houtven / Unsplash; p.171 Craig Russell / Shutterstock, Tupungato / Shutterstock; p.193 Michelle Ziling / Unsplash, NMG Network / Unsplash, Ulysse Pointcheval / Unsplash

ISBN 9780316520522

LCCN is on file with the Library of Congress.

10 9 8 7 6 5 4 3 2 1

WOR

Printed in the United States of America